Ghost Fields of Suffolk

A companion volume to
Ghost Fields of Norfolk
also by Roderick McKenzie

Ghost Fields of Suffolk

*History, plans and photographed remains of
28 Suffolk airfields*

Roderick McKenzie

*Dedicated to my mother,
June Rosemary McKenzie*

The Larks Press

Published by the Larks Press
Ordnance Farmhouse, Guist Bottom, Dereham,
Norfolk NR20 5PF
01328 829207
Larks.Press@btinternet.com
Website: www.booksatlarkspress.co.uk

Printed by Newprint and Design,
Garrood Drive, Fakenham, Norfolk

March 2012

British Library Cataloguing–in–Publication Data
A catalogue record for this book is available
from the British Library

ACKNOWLEDGEMENTS

The author would like to thank the following for their assistance:

Airfield Information Exchange; Bentwaters Cold War Museum; Ipswich Transport Museum; Norfolk & Suffolk Aviation Museum; Parham Airfield Museum; Rougham Tower Association

Special thanks to Ray Bowden of the USAAF Nose Art Research Project (www.usaaf-noseart.co.uk)

Thanks to Jason Himpson, for providing the initial impetus for this project, and thanks, as ever, to Carolyn, for prompting me to actually finish it.

Front cover: Restored Control Tower at Rougham

ISBN 1 904006 60 2

PREFACE

In Hollywood, they talk of 'Development Hell', that place where projects become hopelessly stuck, sometimes for ever. Something similar happened with the volume you now hold: begun back in 2007 as a collaborative effort, it was at a very advanced stage when one of the co-authors abruptly deserted, leaving the manuscript in limbo for the best part of two years. It took the rather peculiar combination of imminent redundancy and an off-the-cuff remark at a family gathering (largely alcohol-inspired), to put the project suddenly back on the map. That in turn led to a rather frantic four weeks of summer field-research by train and bicycle, beginning with roasting temperatures at Rougham, winding up in freezing rain at Felixstowe, and appropriately concluding with being blown away (literally) by a Beech Staggerwing at Little Gransden. If nothing else, it has been an adventure, and I hope you, the readers, derive as much enjoyment from reading it as I have in putting it together.

Rod McKenzie
North Wootton
February 2012

Bibliography

Berry, Paul – *Airfield Heyday* (Privately published, 1989)

Bowyer, Michael J. F. – *Action Stations 1: East Anglia* (PSL 1990)

Ethell, Jeffrey L. & Simonson, Clarence –*The History of Aircraft Nose Art* (Foulis/Haynes 1991)

Faux, Melanie J & Sullivan, Jane (Editors) – *The Reunion 1942-1992* (East Anglia Tourist Board, 1992)

Francis, Paul – *Military Airfield Architecture* (PSL 1996)

Freeman, Roger – *Airfields of the Eighth, Then and Now* (After the Battle, 1978)

Freeman, Roger – *The Mighty Eighth War Manual* (Janes 1984)

Freeman, Roger – *The Mighty Eighth in Colour* (Arms & Armour 1991)

Freeman, Roger – *The B17 Flying Fortress Story* (Arms & Armour 1998)

Gunston, Bill – *Aircraft of World War 2* (St Michael 1983)

Innes, Graham Buchan – *British Airfield Buildings of the Second World War* (Midland 1995)

Innes, Graham Buchan – *British Airfield Buildings: Expansion & Inter-war Periods* (Midland 2000)

Jefford, Wing Commander C. G. – *RAF Squadrons* (Airlife 1988)

Mclachlan, Ian – *Eighth Air Force Bomber Stories* (Sutton 2004)

Skeels, Duncan R. – *Airfields of Suffolk* (Babergh District Council 1997)

Smith, Graham – *Suffolk Airfields in the Second World War* (Countryside 1995)

GHOST FIELDS OF SUFFOLK

Introduction

They called it the 'Friendly Invasion'. It began in the spring of 1942 and reached its zenith around D-Day 1944, by which time there were over 400,000 American airmen stationed in England, the vast majority crammed into a dense network of East Anglian airfields stretching north into Lincolnshire, west to Northamptonshire and south into Essex. This area became known in WW2 as 'Little America', and Suffolk was at its very heart.

Between 1939-45 there were 32 operational military airfields in Suffolk, of which no less than 23 were actually constructed during the conflict (as a point of comparison, neighbouring Norfolk boasted 37 wartime airfields, but these were spread over a much greater geographical area). There was to be a permanent or temporary American presence at nineteen of these sites, and the association between Suffolk and the States would continue through the Cold War and beyond: indeed, it remains strong even as we face the uncertain world of the 21st century.

Suffolk did not have quite the same deep-rooted association with military aviation as did Norfolk, where the Royal Flying Corps had begun operations as early as 1911. That said, a site near Hadleigh was used as a training station in WW1, while Felixstowe and Martlesham Heath could also trace their origins to the formative years of air combat. The latter two sites played a key role in the development of new aircraft types and weapons in the inter-war years.

The 1930s were a time of great uncertainty in continental Europe, and it was fortunate for the fate of civilisation that the RAF chose this period to undertake an ambitious programme of expansion and modernisation. In Suffolk, this 'Expansion Era' produced initially Mildenhall, then later Honington, Stradishall and Wattisham: the signature steel-framed, brick-built C-type hangars becoming a familiar sight throughout rural East Anglia. Thanks to this far-sighted effort, the RAF was ready – albeit only just – for the outbreak of war in 1939.

One realm in which Suffolk made an absolutely vital contribution was the development of radar. Preliminary work on this radical technology was undertaken at the remote Orford Ness site, which had been used for experimental flight-testing in the Great War (and after WW2 would play a key role in the development of Britain's nuclear arsenal). In 1936 the Air Ministry purchased Bawdsey Manor and its surrounding 168-acre estate to develop the first RAF Radio Direction Finding school, and in May 1937 the first radar station came on-line at the site. The network of radar stations constructed around the coast of southern England – known as *Chain Home* – played a crucial role in the Battle of Britain, identifying approaching Luftwaffe raiders and enabling Fighter Command to concentrate its thinly-stretched resources precisely where they were needed most. An important part of the *Chain Home* system was a site at Trimley Heath, which came under control of 11 Group based at North Weald in Essex.

When George Orwell renamed Great Britain as 'Airstrip One' in his seminal novel *1984*, the experience of the Second World War must have been fresh in his mind. During the conflict, in excess of 400 new airfields were constructed, a building programme scarcely conceivable to the modern mind. At the peak point in 1942, a new airfield was opening every three days, with the highest concentration of these new sites being in East Anglia.

As noted, the majority of these new airfields were built for the Americans, who formally entered the war in late 1941, after tacitly supporting the British – both morally and materially – since the beginning. The commitment to defeat Nazi Germany prior to attacking the Japanese homelands, and to do it primarily by strategic bombing, saw the arrival in English shires of an air armada unmatched in history. Men (and later, a significant number of women) began arriving in their thousands, travelling by ocean liner and running the gauntlet of marauding U-boats, or flying the so-called Great Circle Route via Newfoundland, Greenland and Iceland. The 8th Air Force was to be the hammer with which the USAAF (still very much an army unit) bludgeoned the enemy by day, while RAF Bomber Command did much the same at night. Thus was Germany's military and industrial infrastructure dismantled, piece-by-piece, 24/7.

At peak strength in December 1944, the 8thAF marshalled a force of 2,800 heavy bombers and 1,400 escort fighters. In addition there were elements of the tactically inclined 9th and 12th Air Forces, who would make their mark during the liberation of Europe and in the Mediterranean theatre, respectively. The need for escort fighters was demonstrated right from the 8th's first missions in 1942, as the Luftwaffe proved more than reluctant to let their homeland be bombed into smithereens. Fighters and flak exacted an appalling toll on American bombers, and the problem of protecting them was not completely solved until the advent of the P51 Mustang, a phenomenal blending of American and British technology. By its end in May 1945, the campaign to defeat Nazi Germany had cost the lives of some 40,000 American airmen, a sacrifice starkly depicted by the glass Memorial Wall outside Duxford's American Air Museum. For many of these young men, their final resting place was to be the American Cemetery at Madingley, near Cambridge – a long way from home.

Bomber Command's war was no less harrowing. After early daylight operations proved catastrophic failures, they were obliged to develop a whole new ethos, operating under cover of night. However the risks were not significantly reduced in darkness, as the Luftwaffe operated a sophisticated radar system of their own, guiding a lethally effective night-fighter force. Over the target, searchlights and deadly accurate flak accounted for bombers rendered all but helpless on their bombing runs. Bomber Command's eventual losses ran in excess of 10,000 aircraft, at a cost of over 50,000 lives, in a campaign whose merits have long been debated, and whose military significance has only been recognised relatively recently.

The end of WW2, in Suffolk as elsewhere, saw an immediate decline in the number of airfields. However, the onset of the Cold War ensured that the county's military significance would be undiminished. The RAF maintained a strong presence as it headed into the Jet Age, though chillingly this would eventually involve the deployment of Thor nuclear missiles throughout East Anglia. In the 1950s the now independent United States Air Force committed itself to the defence of the United Kingdom, eventually concentrating its resources at the twin bases of Bentwaters and Woodbridge, along with Lakenheath and Mildenhall. The bonds forged between the Americans and the local community were celebrated and strengthened by regular air shows, the most significant being Mildenhall's Air Fête which marked the American Bicentennial in 1976 and continued annually until the end of the millennium. Easily the largest event held in East Anglia, Air Fête regularly attracted crowds in excess of 300,000 to the sleepy heart of rural Suffolk. Sadly, the dreadful events of September 11th 2001 caused the shutters to come down at Mildenhall, and the site does not currently welcome casual visitors, although at the time of writing tentative plans are afoot to bring back some form of public event.

The collapse of the Soviet Union ended the Cold War in a most indecisive manner, and immediately resulted in a further drawing down of military forces in the UK. The Americans abandoned Bentwaters and Woodbridge, leaving Lakenheath (F15 fighter-bombers) and Mildenhall (KC135 tankers) as their final redoubts in Suffolk. The RAF presence has diminished even further, with Honington home to the RAF Regiment but no flying units. Happily, the Army Air Corps remains in strength, basing its sinister Apache helicopters at Wattisham.

Given this rich history, it is gratifying to see how the people of Suffolk have taken steps to preserve the aviation heritage of their county, in marked contrast to neighbouring Norfolk. There is a wealth of memorials and museums, with wartime buildings being actively restored, and even some airfield sites being reactivated, albeit only occasionally. Whereas, in the main, these locations have quite rightly reverted to agriculture, the roar of bombers replaced by birdsong, that of fighters by the fluttering of harvest fields, there can be little doubt that memories of the past remain vibrant in Suffolk, which can only bode well for its future.

A typical wartime airfield

The construction of the many hundreds of airfields that appeared during the Second World War was initially entrusted to civilian contractors, including such familiar names as Laing, McAlpine and Wimpey, but by 1942 these were augmented by Engineering Battalions of the US Army. The standard airfield type was known as 'Class A', intended for heavy bombers but ultimately used by all types of aircraft. This consisted of three concrete runways, the main being 2,000yds long and 50yds wide and aligned with the prevailing wind, plus two subsidiaries 1,400yds long, forming an 'A' pattern. A three-mile long, 50ft wide perimeter track connected these runways, and around this would be arranged up to fifty dispersal points, of either the 'frying-pan' or 'loop' types.

A Control Tower ('Watch Office' in RAF parlance) of brick-faced concrete construction overlooked the runways, traditionally a two-storey building with a frontal viewing balcony and a dedicated weather station atop its flat roof. In the immediate vicinity would be a night-flying equipment store and fire tender shed. The airfield would normally be equipped with at least two aircraft hangars, most commonly of the mass-produced 'T2' type (T for Transportable), and these would frequently be augmented by simple curved-roof 'blister' hangars and prefabricated Robin sheds.

A dedicated trackway, its path denoted by the presence of heavily-fortified fuzing points, led to the bomb dump which was normally dispersed in nearby woodland. The heart of airfield activity would be the Technical Site, where could be found the operations block, bomb-sight store, MT (Motor Transport) section, parachute store and workshops, as well as various buildings dedicated to the training of pilots, bomb-aimers and air gunners. Virtually all of these structures were of brick-faced concrete construction, and intended to last no more than ten years; that so many have survived to the present is an enduring testament to their design.

Chastening experiences with the Expansion Era airfields meant that, as far as practical, the various airfield sub-sites were widely dispersed, accommodation sites being the extreme example. These could be situated anything up to three miles from the main airfield site, and often consisted of little more than mass-produced concrete huts, mainly of the semicircular Nissen and Romney types - such buildings were extremely uncomfortable places to live, especially in winter. High-level Braithwaite water tanks were a regular feature, erected in order to generate sufficient water pressure. Other dispersed locations included the fuel stores, of which there were normally two, built underground and holding 100,000 gallons of aviation spirit apiece, and the communal site, comprising buildings such as the mess hall, gymnasium (which frequently doubled as a chapel and cinema), squash courts and various airmen's services.

In terms of materials, the building of such a massive concern produced appropriately impressive numbers: 175,000 cubic yards of concrete, 32,000 square yards of tarmac, twenty miles of drains and up to four-and-a-half million bricks. The complete airfield – flying surfaces plus supporting buildings – would cost around £1 million, a ferocious sum of money in the 1940s. It was from these frequently bleak installations that British, Commonwealth and American flyers – plus a significant number of escapees from occupied Europe – went to war, with nothing less than the future of humanity in the balance. Many were destined never to return, but upon their sacrifice rests the freedom that today we all too easily take for granted.

Map of Suffolk's Lost Airfields

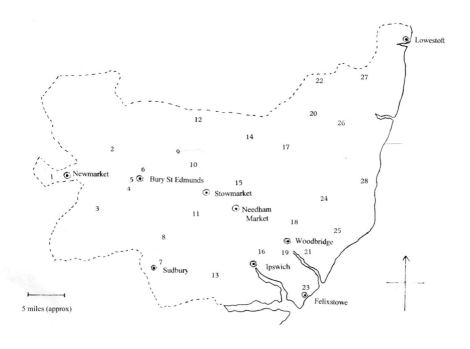

Key to Map

1. Newmarket
2. Tuddenham
3. Stradishall
4. Chedburgh
5. Westley
6. Bury St Edmunds/Rougham
7. Sudbury
8. Lavenham
9. Shepherd's Grove
10. Great Ashfield
11. Rattlesden
12. Knettishall
13. Raydon
14. Eye
15. Mendlesham
16. Ipswich/Nacton
17. Horham
18. Debach
19. Martlesham Heath
20. Metfield
21. Woodbridge
22. Bungay
23. Felixstowe
24. Framlingham/Parham
25. Bentwaters
26. Halesworth
27. Beccles
28. Leiston

BECCLES

The south-east corner of Beccles, with two runways visible:
in the foreground is the former NE-SW runway, and beyond,
the section of E-W runway still used by light aircraft

Construction of Beccles (also known locally as Ellough) began in August 1942, at the height of the new airfield frenzy, and it was pressed into service as an emergency landing ground while still being built. Intended for the USAAF, it was not taken on, also being rejected by RAF Bomber Command before finally being adopted by Coastal Command. Despite an operational career lasting little more than a year, the site was to accumulate a fascinating history.

The first occupants – in August 1944 – were graceful De Havilland Mosquitoes of 618 sqn. This was the sister squadron to the rather better known 617 – the immortal 'Dambusters'. 618 were tasked with developing *Highball*, a smaller anti-shipping version of *Upkeep*, the famous 'Bouncing Bomb'. However, unlike its counterpart *Highball* proved unsuccessful, and was never deployed operationally.

By October 618 had moved on, and Fleet Air Arm assets began to appear at Beccles, led by 827sqn operating the Fairey Barracuda on convoy patrol duties. Though a capable dive/torpedo bomber, the Barracuda acquired a grim reputation due to early design faults causing several fatal accidents. Coastal Command activities at this time switched to air-sea rescue, with squadrons employing a variety of aircraft highlighted by the Supermarine Sea Otter amphibian, the last biplane to be used by the RAF. In April 1945, just weeks before the end of the War in Europe, 810sqn FAA deployed its Barracudas against German midget submarines.

Beccles closed as a military airfield at the end of 1945, but was to have a second vigorous career as a helicopter station servicing North Sea oilrigs, mainly with the ubiquitous Sikorsky S61 – civil variant of the mighty Sea King. Helicopter operations were eventually transferred to Norwich Airport (aka Horsham St Faith), but Beccles was still not completely finished with flying. In 1997 a collection of light aircraft previously housed at Swanton Morley took up residence, and Rainair is now a thriving aviation concern.

Many former airfield buildings have been swallowed up in the Ellough Industrial Estate, but a pair of impressive T2 hangars still remains, one of which has recently become a focus of nostalgia by hosting major forties-style Hangar Dances.

Magnificent T2 hangar, one of two still surviving at Beccles

Location

SW of Beccles, S of A146. B1127 bisects the site. Modern airstrip utilises easternmost portion of former E-W main runway (09/27)

14

Operational History

Aug 44 – Oct 44: 618 sqn (Mosquito IV/VI – weapons testing)
Oct 44   : 827 sqn FAA (Barracuda – convoy patrol)
Oct 44 – Oct 45: 280 sqn (Warwick – air-sea rescue)
Feb 45   : 245 sqn (Walrus II, Sea Otter – air-sea rescue)
Mar 45 – Oct 45: 278 sqn (Walrus – air-sea rescue)
Apr 45 – Jun 45: 810 sqn FAA (Barracuda – anti-submarine ops)
Sep 45   : 279 sqn (Warwick, Sea Otter – air-sea rescue)

Note: In May 1945 288 (Anti-aircraft co-operation) sqn detached to Beccles with target-towing Spitfires. However, their presence was never officially recorded.

The former Communal Site at Beccles is now a rather idiosyncratic industrial park. Note the highly appropriate logo.

Part of the Karting Centre at Beccles occupies a fragment of the NE-SW runway.

Distant view of the Operations Block at Beccles. The remains of several Nissen huts can also be seen.

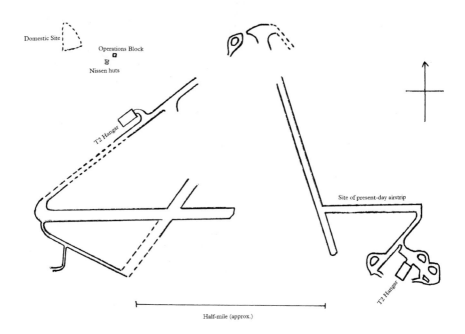

Domestic Site

Operations Block

Nissen huts

T2 Hangar

Site of present-day airstrip

T2 Hangar

Half-mile (approx.)

BENTWATERS

Faded but still proud – the Main Gate sign remains in place at Bentwaters.

This site was originally known as 'RAF Butley', having been briefly used by Sopwith Camels of 230sqn in 1918. Building of a brand-new airfield began in 1942, but work was sporadic and by 1944 the airfield had only seen occasional emergency landings, having like Beccles been passed over by both the USAAF and Bomber Command. Eventually 11 Group Fighter Command took on what was now named Bentwaters, installing a Wing of squadrons flying the inimitable North American Mustang – the 'Cadillac of the Skies'.

The Mustang (American designation P51) was a fighter designed with astonishing swiftness to a British specification. Initially unsuccessful, it became a masterpiece when wedded to the classic Rolls-Royce Merlin engine. Fitted with drop tanks, the Mustang could roam at will over Nazi Germany, instantly solving the problem of escorting daylight bombing raids deep into the enemy homeland.

The Bentwaters Mustang Wing took part in some of the most daring raids of the War's closing months, including strikes on the Gestapo building in Copenhagen (for which they deployed to Fersfield in Norfolk) as well as Hitler's 'Eagle's Nest' and local SS headquarters at Berchtesgaden. Their final mission was in support of the liberation of Guernsey.

Despite having only fleeting participation in the Second World War, Bentwaters was to be a key player in the Cold War (along with nearby Woodbridge, with which it was 'twinned' in July 1958). In 1951 the USAF's 81st Tactical Fighter Wing arrived to begin forty years of continuous operations employing a range of classic American jets, commencing with the F86 Sabre and concluding with the A10 Thunderbolt II, more familiarly known as the 'Warthog'. Down the years other USAF units were to be seen, most significantly (in the late 1980s) the 527th Aggressor Squadron with their F16 Fighting Falcons. Structured and operated along the lines of a Soviet fighter unit, the 527th provided realistic threat training, at least until the USSR abruptly ceased to exist.

An extensively modified wartime T2 hangar which in the airfield's latter years was capable of servicing up to 12 A-10 'Warthogs' at a time

18

Despite this rich history, the single most famous, or infamous, occasion associated with Bentwaters occurred over three nights from December 26th – 29th 1980. The so-called 'Rendlesham Forest Incident' is regarded as one of the major UFO encounters in history, involving significant numbers of USAF personnel from both Bentwaters and Woodbridge. Despite a slew of books, eyewitness testimony and the release of classified official documents, no definitive truth has so far emerged, leaving all explanations – genuine 'close encounter', mistaken identity, hoax – equally valid.

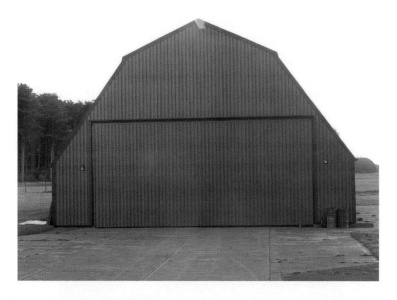

Victor Alert ('Dutch') Barn aircraft shelter designed to make the airfield less obvious to attacking aircraft. At the time of writing this example housed an airworthy Spitfire T9.

The end of the Cold War also meant the end for many USAF bases, Bentwaters among them, and the site closed on July 1st, 1993. Today the technical site is in industrial usage, while the flying field is leased for storage and occasional film work. Of greater note, in 2003 a Cold War Museum was established in the heavily fortified former Command Post. The museum continues to develop, and offers an intriguing insight into a tense period of history when eastern England, along with most of western Europe, stood on the 'front line' between jousting superpowers.

Operational History

Dec 44 – May 45: 129 sqn (Mustang III / Spitfire IXe – bomber escort)

Dec 44 – Aug 45: 64 sqn (Mustang III – bomber escort)

Dec 44 – Aug 45: 118 sqn (Spitfire IXc / Mustang IV – bomber escort)

Dec 44 – Sep 45: 126 sqn (Mustang III,IV – bomber escort)

Dec 44 – May 45: 165 sqn (Mustang III / Spitfire IXe – bomber escort)

Dec 44 – May 45: 234 sqn (Mustang III,IV – bomber escort)

May 45 – Aug 45: 65 sqn (Mustang IV – bomber escort)

Sep 45 – Feb 46: 234 sqn (Spitfire IX – fighter)

Apr 46 – Sep 46: 56 sqn (Meteor F.3 – fighter)

Jun 46: 74 sqn (Meteor F.3 – fighter)

Jun 46: 245 sqn (Meteor F.3 – fighter)

Mar 51 – Mar 93: 81st TFW, USAF (F86A Sabre, F86D Sabre-Dog, F84F Thunderstreak, F4C Phantom II, A10A Thunderbolt II - tactical fighter ops)

Jul 51 – Dec 52: 9th ARS, USAF (SB-29 'Super Dumbo' - air-sea rescue)

Mar 52 – Dec 52: 7554th TTF, USAF (TB-26C Invader, L5E Sentinel – target towing)

Jun 88 – Nov 89: 527th AS, USAF (F16C Fighting Falcon – aggressor tactics)

This Security Checkpoint regulated access to the Weapons Storage Area. The gates to the right were strictly sequenced so that vehicles and pedestrians were trapped in a potential fire zone while their credentials were checked.

Location
SE of Rendlesham, S of A1152 Woodbridge road.

Bentwaters' superb Control Tower with the classic Cold-War era Visual Control Room, or 'glasshouse' added (drawing 5871C/55)

Under a threatening sky, the former Weapons Storage Area at Bentwaters, originally designed to accommodate nuclear ordnance.

Patrons queue to enter the former Command Post at Bentwaters, now the home of the Cold War Museum.

The former Fire Section is now a film and TV production centre.

*The restored interior of the Command Post, designed to handle
tactical nuclear operations*

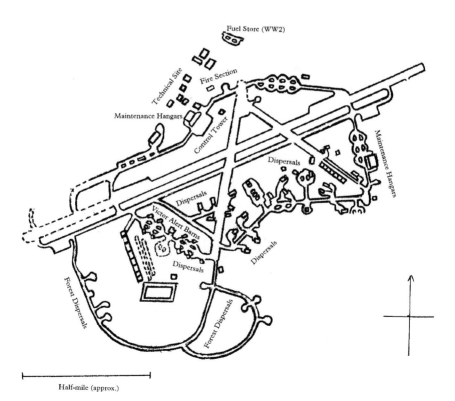

BUNGAY (FLIXTON)

The most intact section of Bungay is shown here, with a taxiway on the left and the remains of the Operations Block and attendant Bombsight Store to the right. This view looks west.

Like so many wartime Suffolk airfields, Bungay was to spend its entire operational career under the control of the United States Army Air Force, and also like so many it was colloquially referred to by another name, in this case Flixton.

In 1942 the first arrivals were B25 Mitchells of the 310th Bombardment Group. The Mitchell – named for the notorious air power advocate, General Billy Mitchell – was a rugged medium bomber and would become an RAF mainstay, but the Americans were strangely reluctant to deploy it from UK soil. Indeed, the 310th were eventually transferred to the 12thAF for service in North Africa.

In December, a squadron of the Hardwick-based 93rd BG – the 329th – arrived, flying an aircraft that was to become synonymous with East Anglia: the Consolidated B24 Liberator. Though never a thing of beauty, especially compared to its more famous counterpart, the B17, the Liberator nonetheless was the most widely produced American heavy bomber of the War, over 19,000 eventually contributing to the Allied victory.

The 329th BS undertook clandestine *Moling* or intruder raids, designed to confuse and harass the German air raid warning system. They also

24

conducted development work on the new radar navigational aid known as *Gee*. After their return to Hardwick in March 1943, further work was carried out on Bungay airfield, expanding the site.

In November the 446th BG – to be known to the ages as the 'Bungay Buckeroos' – took up residence, and Bungay finally joined the great daylight war of attrition against Nazi Germany. The B24s of the 446th would conduct 273 missions, with an impressively low loss rate of 58 aircraft in combat, plus another 28 to other causes. They raided the gruelling targets of Bremen and Brunswick, and attacked V-weapon sites in Northern France on so-called *Noball* missions. On June 6th 1944 they led the first of the Eighth Air Force's many attacks in support of the D-Day invasion.

The delightful 446th BG memorial at Bungay

The 446th carried out their final operation on April 25th 1945, and by June had returned to the United States. Bungay was used to store surplus ordnance until 1955, and was eventually sold off in 1961. However, civil aviation lingered, and there were even a few charity air shows organised in the early 1980s. Today the site is mostly returned to agriculture, although a few buildings remain, but the area of Bungay/Flixton still looms large in the minds of aviation enthusiasts as the home, since 1972, of the Norfolk & Suffolk Aviation Museum. In over 30 years this establishment has grown from literally a handful of aircraft in a pub garden to one of the major museums of its type in the country. Appropriately, one section documents, and commemorates, the achievements of the 'Buckeroos'.

A restored Nissen hut at Flixton now houses the 446th BG Museum

Operational History

Oct 42 – Nov 42: 428th BS/310th BG USAAF (B25C Mitchell - medium bombing)

Dec 42 – Mar 43: 329th BS/93rd BG USAAF (B24D Liberator – radar ops/trials)

Nov 43 – Jun 45: 446th BG USAAF (B24H,J,L,M Liberator – heavy bombing)

Agricultural machinery occupies the former NE-SW runway.

Crash site memorial at Barsham, roughly 3 miles east of Bungay.

Location
E of Flixton, S of B1062 Flixton road

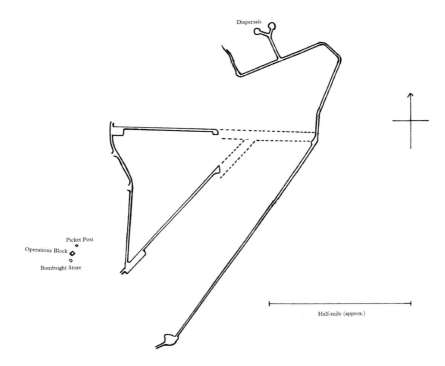

BURY ST EDMUNDS / ROUGHAM

The superbly restored Control Tower at Rougham. The Nissen huts visible to the left have been rescued from other airfield sites for adding to the museum complex. To the right can be seen the Radar/Radio shed, now a canteen.

Nowadays it is universally known as Rougham airfield, and indeed this is what it was originally christened. However, for most of WW2 the site was named for the large town lying just to the west – Bury St Edmunds.

Rougham will be forever associated with that most classic of American bombers, the Boeing B17 Flying Fortress, as incarnated by the 94th Bomb Group who arrived in June 1943, and by their departure in December 1945 had accumulated an astonishing 324 combat missions. But before the arrival of the 94th, two other lesser known, but nonetheless notable, American aircraft types were to be seen at the field.

First was the Douglas A20 Havoc – known to the RAF as the Boston – a pugnacious twin-engine bomber that was hugely effective at low level. Havocs of the 47th BG were briefly based at Rougham in September 1942, before moving on to Horham. In December the 322nd BG took up residence, flying one of those select wartime types worthy of the appellation 'beautiful' – the Martin B26 Marauder.

Amid a sea of ripening corn stands the distinctive shape of an AML Turret Trainer. The interior would have contained a mock-up of a gun turret, facing a huge screen onto which spotlight 'targets' would be projected for the instruction of air gunners.

With its shark-like fuselage, high wings and elegant tail, the Marauder looked so good it is little wonder the US Army Air Corps ordered the type straight off the drawing board. It is also little wonder that this led to a number of potentially fatal teething troubles that had to be ironed out when the aircraft was already in service.

Not helping the Marauder's already grim reputation was the insistence on using it in a low-level role, for which it was far less suited than the Havoc. The loss of one aircraft during practise flights over East Anglia in the spring of 1943 gave some hint of the trouble to come. On 14th May the 322nd launched its first strike against the Ijmuiden power station – nine of twelve B26s despatched sustained heavy flak damage in a raid judged to be a dismal failure. Three days later a second attempt proved even more disastrous: out of a force of eleven bombers, ten failed to return.

Despite such catastrophes, the Marauder was eventually to become a most formidable weapon, which would reach its zenith when the 322nd, along with other medium bomber units, was transferred to the 9th Air Force and departed for Andrew's Field (aka Great Saling) in Essex, and ultimately, tactical forward fields in France. One 322nd aircraft, the provocatively named *Flak Bait,* survived no less than 202 missions, and is now enshrined in the National Air & Space Museum, Washington DC.

Thus by the summer of '43, Rougham reverberated to the roar of heavy bombers, as the 94th BG brought B17s to Bury. Boeing's masterpiece evolved from the radical Model 299 of 1935, the first American four-engine bomber design. The number of defensive machine-gun positions on early B17s led to the popular soubriquet 'Flying Fortress', which was to become only more appropriate as time went on. The Fortress was to be the means by which Billy Mitchell's concept of 'impregnable' mass bomber formations would be tested, and found wanting, in actual combat. Victory would ultimately validate the policy, and turn the B17 into a legend, but not before a terrible price had been paid in men and machines.

The 94th earned two Distinguished Unit Citations during its time at Rougham. The first was for the 'shuttle' raid on Regensburg, 17th August, a gruelling mission involving passage over vast swathes of enemy territory, and persistent fighter attacks, before finally landing in northern Africa. The second followed an attack on the Messerschmitt assembly plant at Waggum, 11th January 1944, which the 94th pressed despite the main bomber force being recalled short of the target, due to weather. Unfortunately the Group lost seven aircraft that day, out of a total 153 lost on operations, plus another 27 to other causes. The airfield itself was to see combat on the night of 3rd-4th March 1945, suffering an intruder attack by Me410s.

Rougham was disposed of in 1948, the flying surfaces reverting to agriculture and its technical site giving way to an industrial estate. However, against the odds, the control tower survived, and eventually became the focus of efforts to preserve the history of the area. The Rougham Tower Association was formed in 1993 and has since performed miracles, not only restoring the tower to its former glory, and creating a museum complex around it, but also bringing Rougham back to life as an airfield. For a few weekends a year, aircraft are permitted to return, activities culminating in a major airshow every August. But keeping such historic sites intact is an on-going struggle; just recently Rougham field has been under threat from a proposed road development. It would be tragic if, after surviving so much, this strip of living history were to be obliterated in the misguided name of 'progress'.

Operational History

Sep 40 – Apr 41: 268 sqn (Lysander II – army co-operation)

Apr 41 – Jul 41: 241 sqn (Lysander III – army co-operation)

Sep 42 – Nov 42: 47th BG USAAF (A20 Havoc – light bombing)

Dec 42 – Jun 43: 322nd BG USAAF (B26B Marauder – medium bombing)

Jun 43 – Dec 45: 94th BG USAAF (B17F,G Flying Fortress – heavy bombing)

The unusual memorial at Rougham incorporates a propeller and part of a Wright Cyclone engine, salvaged from a B17 crash site.

A significant number of buildings still stand at Rougham. Pictured here is the Dinghy Store (nearest camera) and the Parachute Store with its distinctive raised roof containing a central railing for the hanging of parachutes.

Location
E of Bury St Edmunds, N of A14. General Castle Way accesses former Technical Site. Perkins Road & Woodlands Road partly occupy the Perimeter Track.

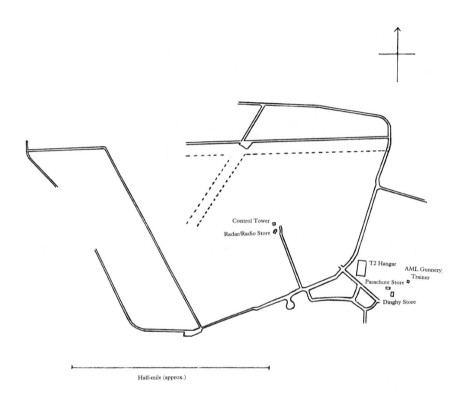

Control Tower
Radar/Radio Store
T2 Hangar
AML Gunnery Trainer
Parachute Store
Dinghy Store

Half-mile (approx.)

CHEDBURGH

A view from the north side Perimeter Track, looking south-east along the former NW-SE runway. The windsock just visible to the left marks the location of Chedburgh's heavily modified Watch Office.

Chedburgh opened in September 1942 as a satellite to Stradishall, and like its parent station is indelibly associated with RAF heavy bombers – in this case, the magnificent but ill-fated Short Stirling.

The early years of the War proved a time of painful transition for Bomber Command. The concept of the light, day bomber, so in vogue during the thirties, had been proven hopelessly flawed during the Battle of France; meanwhile attempts at strategic bombing in daylight were resisted, to lethal effect, by the Luftwaffe. The switch to a night bombing campaign was a challenge both for the crews and for the then generation of RAF 'heavies'. In 1938 the Stirling had been a potentially world-beating design, but desperately compromised by the Air Ministry's insistence on a maximum 99ft wingspan (to suit the C-type hangars then in use). This resulted in poor performance at high level, and the consequences are starkly illustrated by Chedburgh's Stirling squadrons, 214 & 620.

A total of 83 bombers were eventually lost on operations from Chedburgh, no less than 71 of them being Stirlings, and an appalling 50 of these were from 214 sqn. It was not until the arrival of the legendary Avro Lancaster that Bomber Command was able to prosecute fully its nocturnal war of attrition, relegating the Stirling to less aggressive but nonetheless vital roles such as glider-tug and transport. Indeed Lancasters, in the form of 218 sqn, eventually supplanted Stirlings at Chedburgh, albeit not until very late in the War. In addition to bombing raids, 218 flew food supplies to the Dutch and repatriated British prisoners-of-war.

Though much altered, the Main Stores at Chedburgh survive in industrial use.

The immediate post-war period saw two Polish squadrons, 301 & 304, operate long range transport flights, mostly to the Middle East, with a variety of former heavy bomber types, cementing Chedburgh's association with this class of aircraft. Flying ceased at the end of 1946, and the site was disposed of in 1952. In typical fashion the technical site passed into industrial use and the flying field, despite a brief period of use by crop-dusting aircraft, reverted to agriculture.

Operational history

Oct 42 – Dec 43: 214 sqn (Stirling – heavy bombing)
Jun 43 – Nov 43: 620 sqn (Stirling – heavy bombing)
Nov 43 – Dec 44: 1653 HCU (Stirling – bomber training)
Dec 44 – Aug 45: 218 sqn (Lancaster I,III – heavy bombing)
Sep 45 – Dec 46: 301 sqn (Warwick III, Wellington GR.XIV, Halifax VIII – transport)
Sep 45 – Dec 46: 304 sqn (Warwick III, Wellington GR.XIV, Halifax VIII – transport)

Location
Immediately S of Chedburgh village, on opposite side of A143

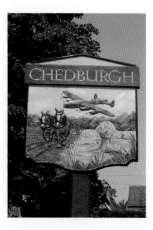

The village sign pays homage the heavy bombers that flew from the nearby airfield

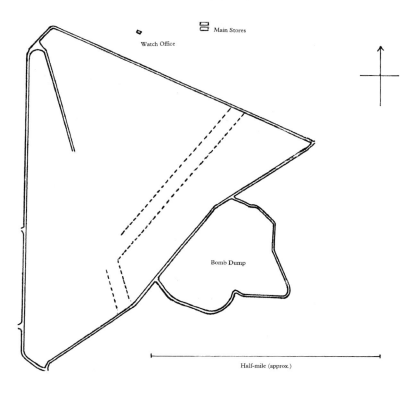

Watch Office

Main Stores

Bomb Dump

Half-mile (approx.)

DEBACH

*The heart of Debach airfield has been beautifully restored: windsock,
Control Tower and a rare example of a Flying Control Trailer
(centre with chequerboard pattern).*

Aviation buffs and historians will likely forever debate the relative merits of
the 8th Air Force's two types of heavy bomber, the Fortress and the
Liberator. However, many of the Bomb Groups based at Suffolk airfields
were able to make a direct comparison, switching from B24s to B17s in line
with Third Air Division policy. One such was the 493rd BG, based at
Debach.

Arriving in April 1944, the 493rd was the last of forty 8thAF Bomb
Groups to become operational in England. The airfield that was to be their
home had been sporadically, and rather poorly, constructed by US Army
engineers; runway problems necessitated a temporary closure at the end of
the year.

Nicknamed 'Helton's Hellcats' after their commanding officer, Col.
Elbert Helton, the 493rd commenced operations on the most momentous
day imaginable – D-Day, 6th June. It was not a great start: two aircraft
were lost in a mid-air collision, but the Group had done its part to support
the Normandy invasion, joining a staggering force of over 2500 bombers
launched by the 'Mighty Eighth' that day.

After 47 missions with B24s, the switch to B17s was rapidly carried out over the period August-September 1944. It was soon after this transition – 11th September – that the 493rd was to suffer its greatest reversal: on a strike against industrial targets in the Ruhland the Group lost ten bombers, of which seven were shot down. Their final tally over 162 combat operations would be 41 aircraft lost, at a cost of 234 lives.

Technical site buildings still in situ at Debach: Dinghy Store (nearest camera) and Parachute Store. Note the slight difference in the arrangement of these same buildings at Bury/Rougham.

In the immediate post-war period Debach was used, somewhat ironically, as a holding camp for German POWs, and later as a temporary refuge for persons displaced by the conflict that had engulfed the whole of Europe. Today, happily, the history of this site is being actively preserved: the Control Tower has been restored as a museum, with other buildings being worked on. A regular programme of events, including 'hangar' dances and an annual 'War & Peace' show, ensure that memories of the 'Hellcats' are kept alive, and vibrant.

Location
S of B1078 Ipswich road; immediately W of Debach hamlet. Drab's Lane passes western edge of field, including Technical Site.

Operational history

Apr 44 – May 45: 493rd BG USAAF (B24J Liberator, B17G Flying Fortress – heavy bombing)

View along the former N-S runway, looking south.

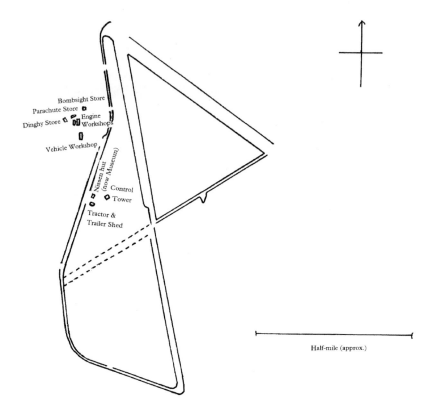

Bombsight Store
Parachute Store
Dinghy Store
Engine Workshops
Vehicle Workshop
Nissen hut (now Museum)
Control Tower
Tractor & Trailer Shed

Half-mile (approx.)

Even modified as a cold store, the frontage of this T2 hangar is unmistakable.

The imposition of 'Little America' upon various sleepy rural backwaters of East Anglia resulted in many intriguing cultural artefacts. The contribution of the 'Friendly Invasion' to wartime Britain was to make it a little brasher, a little louder, a whole lot more colourful, and – it must be said – significantly sexier. And nowhere were colour and sexiness more prevalent than in a form of expression more or less unique to aviation: Nose Art.

The decoration of weaponry with personalised artwork and motifs stretches back to the dawn of civilisation; the onset of the military aeroplane, however, would take the concept to an unprecedented level. Decorated warplanes first appeared over the bloody battlefronts of World War One, but they reached an extraordinary zenith with the USAAF in WW2. Almost every bomber or fighter Group deployed overseas featured or acquired a talented artist to adorn their machines. These transitory artworks – usually executed on the fly, in poor conditions outdoors, and frequently without proper materials – personified the hopes and dreams of young men forcibly displaced from their homes and launched into a most uncertain future. Little wonder, then, that in over 50% of recorded examples, these hopes and dreams took the form of American girls, as idealised by pin-up artists such as George Petty and Alberto Vargas.

Some of the most provocative Nose Art in the entire Army Air Corps was to be witnessed at Eye airfield, home of the 490th BG. It was painted by Sgt Jay Cowan, a man whose story seems to have slipped through the cracks of history, but whose work still makes an impression even in these supposedly more liberated times. On one B17, an unfeasibly voluptuous, naked redhead lay full-length along the nose, accompanied by the legend *£5 With Breakfast* – a blunt reference to the rate of a better-class London prostitute of the day. In another example, *Bobby Sox*, the 'bb' comprised the *derrière* of an athletic, nude, young lady. However it was not all smut: designs such as the southern belle adorning *Alice Blue Gown*, or the crescent-riding nymph of *Carolina Moon*, would be considered magnificent works of art in any context.

The former Gas Clothing & Respirator Store survives in industrial usage.

While many Bomb Groups had their artworks censored either internally or externally, few such strictures appear to have been in place at Eye. Whatever moral laxity this might indicate on the part of the 490th's command staff, there can be little doubt it had a positive effect: over the course of 158 missions, the 490th suffered just 22 combat losses, one of the lowest rates in all the 8thAF.

The 490th arrived at Eye in April 1944, commencing operations the next month with B24 Liberators, before switching to B17s in August, after their 40th mission. Their targets were many and varied, including tactical support of the Normandy invasion, industrial regions of the German heartland, enemy airfields and rail concentrations. One of these latter strikes, on 19th April 1945, showed that, even with the War in Europe all but over, the Luftwaffe still had teeth: an attack by deadly Me262 jet fighters claimed four bombers in what was one of the last aerial engagements fought by the 'Mighty Eighth'.

By August 1945 the 490th and its uniquely adorned Fortresses had departed, and soon after Eye ceased to exist as an airfield. A British Gas installation now occupies part of the site, which has otherwise reverted to the usual mix of agriculture and industry. The 490th has a particularly charming memorial, in the form of a lych-gate at Brome.

Operational history
Apr 44 – May 45: 490th BG USAAF (B24HJ Liberator, B17G Flying Fortress – heavy bombing)

Location
NW of Eye, E of A140. B1077 passes eastern side of Technical Site; industrial park access road leads to Perimeter Track & runways.

An Electrical Sub-station at Eye, still fulfilling its original function.

41

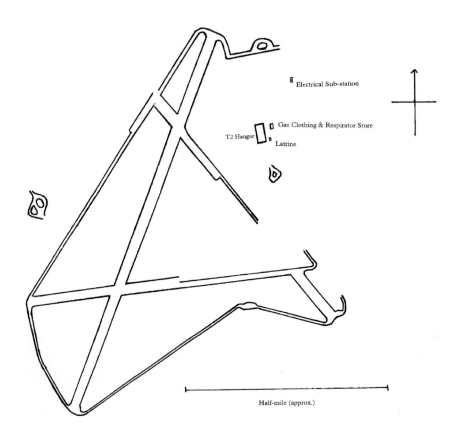

Electrical Sub-station

Gas Clothing & Respirator Store

T2 Hangar

Latrine

Half-mile (approx.)

FELIXSTOWE

A forest of cranes now covers the former site of MAEE Felixstowe. The concrete trackway in the foreground was part of the extensive anti-aircraft installation on Landguard Peninsula.

Before 1918, and the formation of the Royal Air Force, Britain's military air assets were divided between the Army's Royal Flying Corps and the Royal Naval Air Service. This latter organisation naturally tended towards establishments on or near the coast, and the operation of seaplanes. Aircraft that could operate from water, though rarely seen nowadays (especially in this part of the world), were a major strategic asset right through to the end of WW2, and in their ultimate form – the flying boat – were the first expression of the 'global reach' that aviation could provide.

Felixstowe opened in 1913 – a scant ten years after the Wright brothers' first flight - making it the oldest 'airfield' in Suffolk. Under RNAS supervision it was actually responsible for the design of new seaplanes (originally referred to as 'hydro-planes'), the appropriately-named Felixstowe series, which proved a scourge of German U-boats operating in the North Sea during WW1.

Post-war, Felixstowe survived the rapid contraction of the newly formed RAF, and in 1924 became home to the Marine Aircraft Experimental Establishment. Thus a parade of exotic flying boats – many of them unique prototypes – was to be seen in Felixstowe's waters. Perhaps the most exotic was the bizarre Shorts Mayo 'Composite', in effect two flying boats yoked together – the huge long-range *Maia* carrying the fast mail-plane *Mercury* atop its fuselage. Only slightly less freakish was the colossal Short Sarafand, a six-engine monster.

Short Brothers were the undisputed masters of the flying boat, and their crowning achievement was the mighty Sunderland. One of WW2s unsung work-horses, the Sunderland tirelessly patrolled UK waters on anti-submarine patrols. Though seemingly huge and lumbering, it proved a handful for would-be interceptors, earning the nickname 'flying porcupine' from chastened Luftwaffe pilots.

With the onset of war, the MAEE was judged too vulnerable at Felixstowe, and relocated to Helensburgh in Scotland. However, flying boats continued to be seen at the site, including a handful of Fokker T.VIIIs that were remnants of the Netherlands Marine Air Force and eventually became the nucleus of 320 sqn. Sunderlands came for maintenance and modification, as later did their American equivalent, the Consolidated Catalina.

At the end of the War the MAEE returned to Felixstowe, but the era of the flying boat was drawing to a close. The chief attractions were captured German examples, including Bv138s, Do24s and the extraordinary floatplane variant of the Ju52 transport. A disaster in 1946, when the prototype Short Shetland caught fire and sank at its moorings, signalled the beginning of the end, and the MAEE was eventually disbanded in 1958.

In the meantime RAF air-sea rescue assets in the form of 22 sqn's Whirlwind helicopters had arrived at Felixstowe, and there was to be fleeting re-acquaintance with flying boats of a sort, when USAF SA-16 Albatross amphibians undertook training in the adjacent waters. However it was not to last – 22 sqn moved out in May 1961, and Felixstowe closed in August 1962. Today a huge container dock has swallowed up the site, and sadly the last surviving seaplane shed, despite being a listed building, was demolished in 2010.

Crash site memorial at Felixstowe, one of two to be found along the front. Beyond are the waters where mighty flying boats once took off.

Operational history

Aug 18 – May 22: 230 sqn (Curtiss H.16 / Felixstowe F.2A, F.3, F.5 / Short 184 / Fairey IIIB,C – maritime patrol/development)

Aug 18 – Jul 19: 231 sqn (Felixstowe F.2A, F3, F5 – maritime patrol)

Aug 18 – Jan 19: 232 sqn (Felixstowe F.2A, F3 – maritime patrol)

Aug 18 – Jan 19: 247 sqn (Felixstowe F.2A, F3 – maritime patrol)

Mar 31: 203 sqn★ (Fairey IIIF – reconnaissance)

May 31 – Jun 31: 210 sqn (Southampton II – maritime patrol)

May 35 – Aug 39: 209 sqn (Singapore III – maritime patrol)

May 40 – Nov 40: 320 sqn (Fokker T.VIII – maritime patrol)

Jun 55 – Aug 62: 22 sqn★ (Whirlwind – air-sea rescue)

NOTE: In August 1918, two further F.2A squadrons – 259 & 261 - were authorised to form at Felixstowe, but they did not reach operational status.

★indicates detachment only

Location

Felixstowe harbour. Cold Store Road accesses former seaplane site.

This discreet plaque on the wall of Felixstowe Town Hall is one of the few tangible reminders of the former seaplane base. Not far away is another, the delightfully named 'Flying Boat Bar'.

FRAMLINGHAM (PARHAM)

The heart of Framlingham airfield: restored Control Tower with added Nissen huts at left and an intact T2 hangar.

Framlingham was the official name of the airfield built from 1942-43, but the local designation of Parham achieved such wide currency that it is all but universal today. The site would always be associated with B17s, beginning with the 95thBG who arrived in May 1943 for a brief - and disastrous - stay. On 13th June they led an attack on Kiel, over the course of which half the bomber force was wiped out by marauding Luftwaffe fighters. Just two days later the depleted 95th decamped to Horham to regroup, and their place was taken by the 390thBG.

The 390th fought a long and bitter daylight campaign, including shuttle raids to Russia and North Africa, plus assaults on the most feared targets in the 8thAF, including Berlin. Along the way they managed to set some unique milestones, beginning with the brutal Munster raid of 10th October, during which their gunners claimed 60 enemy fighters – the highest single claim of the War. Just four days later, participation in the catastrophic Schweinfurt raid earned the Group a Distinguished Unit Citation.

On 27th December 1944 a bomb-laden B17 crashed in the village of Parham, with a detonation on a scale barely conceivable today. Unsurprisingly, the unfortunate crew perished in the fireball, but miraculously no civilians were killed or even seriously hurt, although every building in Parham sustained damage.

The 390th undertook their final mission on 20th April 1945 – it was their 300th. In the process they had lost 144 aircraft on operations, but from their ranks came a most extraordinary story of survival. Master Sergeant Hewitt Dunn, an air gunner, somehow made it through 104 missions during his time at Framlingham, another 8thAF record.

Quickly abandoned in August 1945, Framlingham's runways were broken up for hardcore, but a number of buildings survived in agricultural and industrial use, and fortunately this remains the case today. Of course, the most iconic building is the Control Tower, which volunteers began restoring in 1976, and which in 1981 was officially dedicated as the 390thBG Memorial Museum.

The view south along Framlingham's former N-S runway.

Operational history
May 43 – Jun 43: 95th BG USAAF (B17F Flying Fortress – heavy bombing)
Jul 43 – Aug 45: 390th BG USAAF (B17F,G Flying Fortress – heavy bombing)

Location
E of Parham, SW of Gt Glenham. New Road runs N-S through middle of site

The magnificently restored Control Tower, seen here playing host to a visiting cycle club (not inappropriate as bicycles were the primary form of personal transport on wartime airfields). Details to note include the signals square and the weather station beyond. On the right side of the building can be seen two memorials, a propeller and a plaque. On the left hand corner of the roof is a replica smoke pot, a device to determine wind direction on poor visibility days.

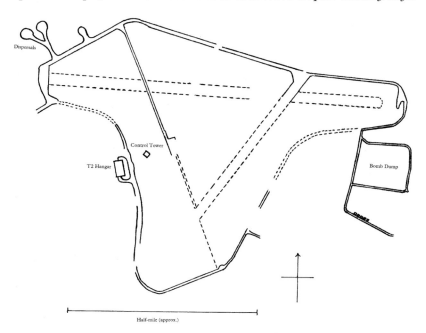

GREAT ASHFIELD

A view from the northern Perimeter Track, looking south-east directly across the airfield. Part of the NW-SE runway can just be seen on the left.

The airfield at Great Ashfield opened in March 1943, although the site upon which it was constructed had been used by the RFC back in the Great War. It was briefly used for practise landings by Bomber Command Stirlings, before being turned over to the USAAF. In June it became home to the 395thBG, nicknamed 'Van's Valiants' for CO, Col. Elliott Van Devanter.

Flying B17s the 385th undertook 290 missions, losing 129 bombers to enemy fire plus another 40 to accidental causes. Of these losses, the most unusual was that of an aircraft named *Powerful Katrinka*, destroyed in a hangar during an intruder attack by a Junkers Ju88 on the night of 22-23rd May 1944. This is believed to be the only instance of a B17 lost to enemy action at its home airfield by the 8thAF. On the credit side, the 385th's gunners claimed 280 Luftwaffe fighters, and the Group earned two Distinguished Unit Citations: first for the Regensburg 'Shuttle' raid, and second for a gruelling attack on the Zwickau aircraft repair plant, 17th May 1944.

Like so many Bomb Groups, the 385th was able to call upon the services of a talented artist to decorate their airplanes. Unusually, the 385th's resident nose artist was a local civilian; even more unusually, the artist was also a woman – Anne Heyward. Rejected by the British Red Cross on account of her Austrian mother, this former art student was determined nonetheless to do her part for the war effort. Taken on by the rather more enlightened American Red Cross, her attractiveness and artistic talent soon made her a permanent fixture at Great Ashfield.

As well as the noses of aircraft, Heyward painted mess hall murals and individual flying jackets, mostly with alluring pin-ups – a demanding workload, even without considering the need to work mostly outdoors and with few proper materials. She occasionally freelanced for other Suffolk-based Bomb Groups, but such was Anne's reputation at Great Ashfield that a B17 was eventually named for her: *Haybag Annie*, which duly racked up 105 combat missions.

Somewhat ironically, the most famous nose art associated with the 385th was not one of Anne Heyward's works. This was *Ruby's Raiders*, named for Pfc Ruby Newell from Long Beach, California, who in late 1944 was voted 'most beautiful WAC' serving in England by *Stars & Stripes* magazine. The artwork - a stunning portrait of Miss Newell - was painted by Cpl William Ploss of the 385th. *Ruby's Raiders* completed at least 20 combat missions, but her ultimate fate is unclear: one source claiming she was lost on 24th March 1945, others that she survived to return to the States.

By June 1945 the 385th had left Great Ashfield, and the airfield fell silent. It was used as a store for surplus bombs before being sold off in 1959. Since then the site has gradually crumbled back into the Suffolk countryside, with little remaining by way of buildings or flying surfaces. However, towards the close of the 20th Century, the ghosts of Great Ashfield were stirred once more, courtesy of a popular television programme.

In June 1998 Channel 4's archaeology show *Time Team* undertook a dig with a difference, excavating the remnants of two 385th B17s that had collided over Reedham Marsh in Norfolk. One of them, *Sleepytime Gal II*, was believed to have been painted by Anne Heyward, and the lady herself was invited to participate in what proved a most poignant excavation.

Anne Heyward is no longer with us, but her artworks live on in photographs, part of the extraordinary folkloric tapestry that was the 'Mighty Eighth's' time in England. 'Van's Valiants' – especially those who gave their lives for freedom – are appropriately commemorated by a memorial altar in Great Ashfield's All Saints church.

Anne Heyward's reconstructed 'Sleepy Time Gal', nose art, as produced for the Time Team programme (now in Norfolk and Suffolk Aviation Museum).

Operational history
Jun 43 – Aug 45: 385th BG USAAF (B17F,G Flying Fortress – heavy bombing)

Location
SE of Great Ashfield, E of Elmswell road.   Haugh Lane & Wheeler's Lane both lead onto the airfield site.

Believed to have been a Barrack Block, this building is one of a handful still extant on the western edge of the airfield.

*A stylised B17 flies above Great Ashfield on the village sign.
Note the 385th BG insignia.*

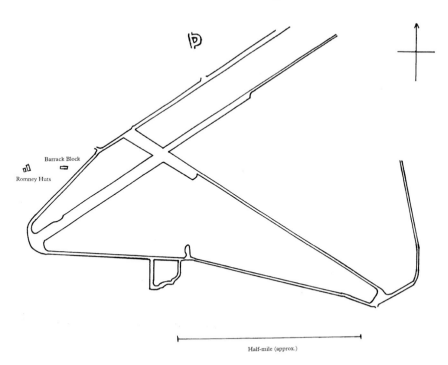

Barrack Block

Romney Huts

Half-mile (approx.)

HALESWORTH

The road in the foreground once formed part of the western Perimeter Track.
The turkey shed beyond occupies part of the former N-S runway.

The turkey sheds that now cover the former runways at Halesworth can only partially obscure a most distinguished history. Construction of the airfield began in 1942, and by July '43 those same, newly-minted runways groaned under the weight of a truly remarkable aircraft: the Republic P47 Thunderbolt, as operated to devastating effect by the USAAF 56th Fighter Group, 'The Wolfpack'.

The P47, also known as the 'Jug' (short for juggernaut) was the largest and heaviest single-engine fighter of the War. First flying in 1941, the Thunderbolt had a lineage dating back to the classic Seversky P35 of the mid-thirties, and was essentially designed around the most powerful engine then available, the Pratt & Whitney R2800 Double Wasp. The result was a fast, tough, brutish fighter that made up in range and firepower what it lacked in elegance and manoeuvrability.

Under Col. Hubert 'Hub' Zemke the 56th FG would become an elite unit, and eventually record the highest number of kills in the 8thAF. Remarkably, they achieved this despite being the only Fighter Group never to convert from P47s to P51 Mustangs, thus demonstrating their absolute mastery of the Thunderbolt as a fighting machine. In April 1944 the 56th moved on to Boxted in Essex, where they would further cement their legend.

In their place came the 489th Bomb Group, flying that other unsung warhorse, the Liberator. The 489th fought a brief and savage campaign before being reassigned to the Pacific Theatre, and from among their ranks came a story of extraordinary courage. On 5th June, the eve of D-Day, Deputy Group Commander Leon R. Vance was leading the Group in a Pathfinder aircraft, to a target near Boulogne. Unfortunately his B24 sustained a direct flak hit, which instantly killed Vance's co-pilot and grievously wounded Vance himself – indeed his right foot was all but severed. Despite this, Vance fought through unimaginable pain to press the attack, and then fly the stricken bomber back to friendly waters so the crew could bale out. Vance, believing there was still at least one crewmember on board, somehow managed to ditch the aircraft, the resulting explosion severing his foot completely. Astonishingly, he then survived almost an hour in the water before a rescue launch found him. Leon R. Vance was awarded the Medal of Honour, but in one of the bitter ironies of war, lost his life when the transport returning him to the US went missing, somewhere in the grey unforgiving seas between Iceland and Newfoundland.

In January 1945 two highly unusual American units arrived at Halesworth. One was a target-towing flight operating the obscure Vultee Vengeance, a former dive- bomber with a dubious reputation. The other was the 5th Emergency Rescue Squadron - a dedicated air-sea rescue unit operating an intriguing mix of aircraft including war-weary P47s, the rare OA-10 variant of the Catalina amphibian, and B17 Fortresses specially modified to carry lifeboats. In February the 496th Fighter Training Group finally brought P51 Mustangs to the airfield. All three units stayed until the close of hostilities.

Unlike so many airfields, Halesworth did not immediately become inactive with the end of the War. Its coastal proximity made it an attractive location for the Fleet Air Arm, who took over in August 1945 and based training units there until early 1946 and the final closure of the site.

Halesworth's rich history is now rightly commemorated by a series of memorials and a museum recently established at the threshold of one of its former runways, demonstrating to the casual visitor that there is far more to this out-of-the-way place than a simple turkey farm.

Operational history

Jul 43 – Apr 44: 56th FG USAAF (P47 Thunderbolt – bomber escort)

Apr 44 – Nov 44: 489th BG USAAF (B24H Liberator – heavy bombing)

Jan 45 – May 45: 1st G&TTF USAAF (A35 Vengeance – target-towing)

Jan 45 – May 45: 5th ERS USAAF (P47 Thunderbolt / OA-10 Catalina / B17 Flying Fortress – air-sea rescue)

Feb 45 – May 45: 496th FTG USAAF (P51D Mustang – fighter training)

Nov 45 – Jan 46: 798 sqn FAA (Barracuda/Oxford – advanced flying training)

Nov 45 – Feb 46: 702 sqn FAA (Beaufort/Oxford – twin conversion training)

Former domestic site dispersed south-east of Halesworth.

Location

N of Holton, E of A144 Norwich road. Sparrowhawk Road adjoins Perimeter Track.

Halesworth's Operations Block still survives, albeit in poor condition.
A Bombsight Store can just be made out in the centre of the picture.

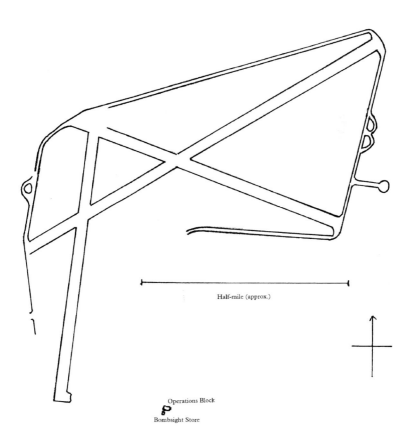

Half-mile (approx.)

Operations Block
Bombsight Store

HORHAM

The view east along Horham's former main runway –
still an impressive sight.

For American servicemen assigned to this airfield, one of the immediate challenges was its name. The local pronunciation of 'Horrum' proved somewhat disconcerting for incomers who had guessed at an altogether more literal (and highly suggestive) interpretation. Building work began in late 1941 and the airfield's early history neatly paralleled Bury/Rougham – first occupants were the 47th BG flying A20 Havocs, followed by the 323rd BG with B26 Marauders. By the summer of 1943 these units had moved on to North Africa and Essex, respectively.

In June the 95th BG – previously noted at Framlingham – arrived with their B17s following a traumatic introduction to the daylight bombing campaign. They rebounded to compile a most distinguished record whilst at Horham, including no less than three Distinguished Unit Citations: for the Regensburg 'shuttle' mission, the Munster raid of 10th October 1943, and the first 8thAF assault on Berlin, 2nd March 1944. These three endeavours cost the Group fourteen aircraft out of a total 157 lost over 320 combat operations. By way of recompense the 95th's gunners claimed 425 enemy fighters shot down.

At the close of hostilities the 95th assisted in dropping food supplies to the Dutch, which resulted in a poignant incident on 7th May 1945. Whether through ignorance or simple spite German ground troops opened fire at a low-flying B17, eventually causing it to ditch with the loss of all but two of the crew. It was the last American bomber lost to enemy action in Europe.

After a brief post-war period of use by RAF maintenance units, Horham officially closed in 1948. However, it was subsequently reactivated to house Bloodhound interceptor missiles and not finally disposed of until the 1960s.

Happily, many of Horham's buildings survive, and are still being put to practical use. The Officers Club has been restored as a function venue, now known as the 'Red Feather Club', while the former Hospital has been turned into a museum and other buildings are being actively restored. Light aircraft still occasionally use the runways, and there is a spectacular memorial to the 95th in Horham village itself.

Operational history

Oct 42 – Jan 43: 47th BG USAAF (A20 Havoc – light bombing)
May 43 – Jun 43: 323rd BG USAAF (B26 Marauder – medium bombing)
Jun 43 – May 45: 95th BG USAAF (B17F,G Flying Fortress – heavy bombing)

Location

NW of Horham, N of B1117. Horham Road crosses surviving runway section.

The restored former Domestic Site to the west of the main airfield. This complex now includes the Red Feather Club.

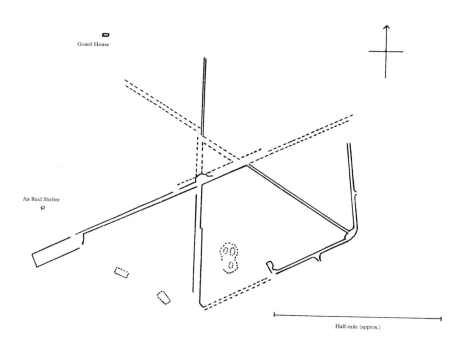

Guard House

Air Raid Shelter

Half-mile (approx.)

An air-raid shelter surviving in good condition at Horham.

Crash site memorial located approximately two miles south of Horham airfield.

IPSWICH (NACTON)

The former Terminal Building at Ipswich has been converted into flats and a community centre. During redevelopment this building was reduced to a façade, and the control cabin atop the roof is a modern replica. Note the large C (for Control) and the propeller motif in the fencing. One other building from the Nacton site survives – a small hangar that originally stood just to the left of the terminal, and is now preserved at Flixton.

The closure of Ipswich Airport – also known as Nacton – in 1998 was not only a blow to General Aviation in the region, but also summarily ended a remarkable history encompassing both peace and war.

No less a person than HRH the Prince of Wales opened the airfield on 26th June 1930, as home of the Suffolk Aero Club. By 1938 quasi-military operations had already commenced with Volunteer Reserve pilots undertaking basic training, and in 1939 the site was officially requisitioned by the Air Ministry. As a satellite to Wattisham it hosted the quintessential RAF aircraft of the early war years – the Bristol Blenheim.

Nowadays known as the 'forgotten bomber', the Blenheim evolved from a one-off executive transport which scandalously, in 1936, proved faster than any contemporary RAF fighter. Adapted as a day bomber, the Blenheim's performance was progressively degraded by the addition of defensive guns and armour plate, so that by the outbreak of war it was already verging on obsolescence, and proved hopelessly outmatched by Luftwaffe fighters. After catastrophic losses the Blenheim was withdrawn from frontline service, but carved out new roles as a night-fighter and in the Mediterranean theatre. The high point of the Blenheim's time at Ipswich was a raid on Cologne, 12th August 1941, for which three squadrons of Spitfires were brought in to provide escort.

From March 1942 to February 1943 Ipswich was transferred to the control of 12 Group, Fighter Command, meaning fleeting visits by a large number of Spitfire squadrons; and then in March '43 came another change: Ipswich became a station in its own right. This meant the disappearance of combat aircraft, but an extraordinary variety of unusual types engaged in lesser known, but crucial, military aviation activities.

For a start there was target towing, for the benefit of naval gunners at nearby Harwich: firstly with the Hawker Henley (another unsuccessful day bomber), and later with the Miles Martinet, a dedicated target tug. Air Observation Post squadrons were also to be seen, flying one of the lightest – and ironically most feared – military aircraft of the War, the delightful Auster III. Even more extraordinary were the C.30a autogyros (aka Rota Is) of 529 sqn, which arrived in November 1944 to undertake calibration flights.

Close proximity to the town that shared its name saw Ipswich involved in a number of attacks. Two in September 1944 involved V1 flying bombs air-launched from Heinkel He111 bombers. The raids caused many casualties but the airfield carried on regardless.

In 1946 Ipswich was returned to civilian control, and for over 50 years was again to be a centre of private flying. Hundreds of pilots earned their fixed-wing and helicopter licenses from the lush grass of Nacton, before sheer greed on the part of local authorities brought it all to an abrupt end. In 1996 the airfield's license was withdrawn, and two years later the last aircraft departed. Since then the site has steadily disappeared under housing developments. Fortunately, Ipswich's wonderful terminal building has been listed, and survives as a reminder of past glories, unnecessarily trampled in the modern age.

Operational history
1938-39: 45 ERFTS (Tiger Moth – flying training)
Aug 39 – Mar 41: 1517 BAT Flt (Oxford – flying training)

May 39 – Mar 41: 107 sqn* (Blenheim IV – day bombing)
Jun 39 – Mar 42: 110 sqn* (Blenheim IV – day bombing)
Mar 41 – May 41: 86 sqn* (Blenheim IV – day bombing)
Apr 41:   268 sqn (Lysander III – Army co-operation)
Nov 41:   287 sqn* (Blenheim IV / Hudson III / Lysander III / Hurricane I,IIb,IV – target towing/gunnery training)
Jun 42:   402 sqn (Spitfire Vb – fighter)
Jul 42:   129 sqn (Spitfire Vb – fighter)
Jul 42:   340 sqn (Spitfire Vb – fighter)
Jul 42:   611 sqn (Spitfire IX – fighter)
Aug 42:   131 sqn (Spitfire Vb – fighter)
Aug 42:   154 sqn (Spitfire Vb – fighter)
Sep 42:   302 sqn (Spitfire Vb – fighter)
Sep 42:   308 sqn (Spitfire Vb – fighter)
Sep 42:   331 sqn (Spitfire Vb – fighter)
Sep 42:   616 sqn (Spitfire VI – fighter)
Mar 43 – Dec 43: 1616 Flt (Henley – target towing)
Apr 43 – Jul 43: 3 AATTF (Henley – target towing)
Jun 43 – Feb 44: 1499 Gunnery Flt (Martinet – target towing)
Jul 43 – Dec 43: 1627 Flt (Henley / Martinet – target towing)
Nov 43 – Mar 44: 652sqn (Auster III – Army co-operation)
Dec 43 – Jun 46: 577 sqn* (Hurricane IIc,IV / Oxford / Beaufighter I / Spitfire Vb, XVI / Vengeance IV – target towing/gunnery training)
Dec 43 – Jun 45: 679 sqn (Henley III / Martinet / Oxford /Hurricane IIc,IV / Barracuda II / Vengeance IV – anti-aircraft/searchlight co-operation)
Mar 44 – May 45: 1696 BDTF (Martinet / Hurricane / Spitfire – bomber defence training)
Nov 44: 529 sqn* (Rota I – instrument calibration)

NOTES: 3 AATFF was absorbed by 1627 Flt in July 1943; 1616 & 1627 Flts were merged in December 1943 to form 679 sqn.

*Indicates detachment only

Location
Ipswich, N of A14.   Nacton Road passes former Terminal building.

Memorial plaque from opening of Ipswich terminal, now preserved at Ipswich Transport Museum. Sixty years after this dedication the last aircraft left the Nacton site and Ipswich Airport ceased to exist.

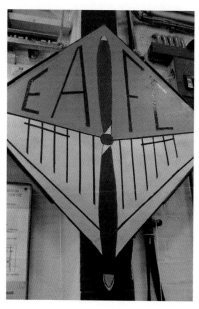

Hand-painted sign of the East Anglia Flying Club, salvaged from Nacton and now also kept at Ipswich Transport Museum.

KNETTISHALL

A view west across the airfield. The former E-W runway is at the left, a fragment of the NW-SE runway in the middle, and the line of the NE-SW runway is just discernible on the horizon.

The airfield at Knettishall opened in January 1943, originally as a satellite to Honington, but was quickly passed to the USAAF and by June was occupied by the B17s of the 388th Bomb Group, who would remain until the close of hostilities.

In many respects the 388th fought a dual war. The first element was that of a conventional 8thAF Bomb Group; they conducted 306 gruelling daylight missions and suffered accordingly, losing 180 aircraft. Distinguished Unit Citations were earned, first for the Regensburg 'shuttle' raid and then for an attack on the Brux oil plant, 12th May 1944. Other targets included names guaranteed to send a shudder through American airmen, such as Berlin and Schweinfurt; as well as less obvious objectives like U-boat pens in southern France.

The other part of the 388th's war was conducted well away from prying eyes, and came in response to a new and fearsome phase of the European conflict signalled in 1944 by the V-1 'flying bomb', first of the so-called 'Revenge' weapons. A squadron of the 388th, the 562nd, was detached and merged with an experimental US Navy unit for the purpose of developing remote-controlled, TV-guided robot bombers to deploy against V-1 launch sites. For added security the 562nd relocated to Fersfield, in deepest Norfolk, where the project, code-named *Aphrodite,* eventually reached operational status. The disastrous early *Aphrodite* missions are detailed in *Ghost Fields of Norfolk,* from the same publisher and author as this volume. Suffice it to say the project was an abject failure, and an eventual return to Knettishall did not improve matters, with only a handful of unsuccessful launches.

With the departure of the 388th Knettishall's career as a military aerodrome ended, though it was not finally disposed of until 1957. Light aviation maintained a presence until fairly recently, including at one stage a sky-diving school, but today the site is purely agricultural. Along with a memorial on the edge of the former airfield, a T2 hangar survives in good condition to remind passers-by of Knettishall's unique role in more turbulent times.

Operational history
Jun 43 – Apr 45: 388th BG USAAF (B17F,G Flying Fortress – heavy bombing)

Location
NE of Coney Weston, NW of B1111. Minor road running S from Knettishall bisects site.

The spectacular memorial to the 388th BG, located on the southern edge of the airfield amid the remains of a Domestic Site.

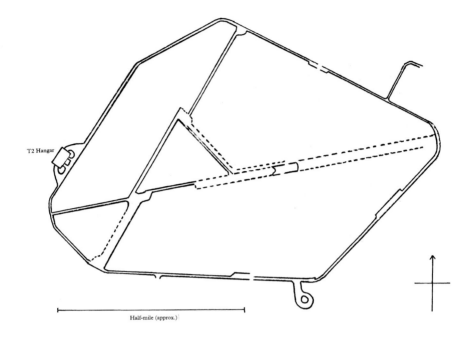

T2 Hangar

Half-mile (approx.)

LAVENHAM

Long in private use, Lavenham's Control Tower overlooks a field mostly returned to agriculture.

Lavenham is a stunningly preserved mediaeval wool town, whose bucolic splendour has made it a major tourist attraction in the modern era. It seems almost unthinkable that such a site should have been involved in the 20th century's most epic conflict, yet a mere three miles to the north, an airfield was constructed in 1943 that would host part of the implacable war machine that was the 'Mighty Eighth'.

They were the 487th BG, who commenced operations in May 1944 with B24 Liberators, switching to B17s in July after 46 missions. They would ultimately conduct 195, a mix of strategic and tactical bombing raids as the European war turned decisively in the Allies' favour. It was one of these latter sorties that produced a story of unimaginable courage and sacrifice – that of Frederick Castle.

The 8thAF mounted its largest ever strike force on 24th December 1944, launching some 2000 bombers in an effort to disrupt the German Ardennes counter-offensive that was then in full swing. Brigadier-General Castle, commander of the 4th Bomb Wing, opted to fly as co-pilot in the 487th's lead aircraft. A surprise attack by Luftwaffe fighters over Allied territory damaged Castle's B17, which fell out of the formation and was immediately set upon by Messerschmitt 109s. With three crew-members badly wounded, Castle took the controls himself and ordered the remainder – including the pilot – to bale out. As he struggled to control the now stricken bomber, yet another attack caused the fuel tanks to explode, sending the flaming wreck spiralling to earth. Castle was posthumously awarded the Medal of Honour. From this raid the 487th lost three B17s shot down, plus another five written off in crash landings, from an eventual total of 48 lost in action.

Post-war Lavenham bounced from RAF Transport Command to Maintenance Command to Bomber Command, yet by 1948 was inactive. However, it briefly sprang to life once more to facilitate filming of the classic war movie *Twelve O'clock High*. Later came sporadic use by crop-dusting aircraft, but today the airfield is silent. The former Control Tower has long been a private dwelling, and a goodly number of other buildings survive. Meanwhile, visitors to Lavenham town can find the 487th remembered in the Market Place and in the Swan Hotel, which was a favourite off-duty haunt of American airmen. They too are now part of the rich historical fabric of this delightful place.

Operational history
Apr 44 – Aug 45: 487th BG USAAF (B24H,J Liberator / B17G Flying Fortress – heavy bombing)

Location
NW of Lavenham, E of A134, W of A1141 Bury road. Gallow Lane and Old Bury Road connect to the Perimeter Track.

Wild flowers make a determined assault on the southern Perimeter Track.

The evocative ruins of the Radar Workshop, to drawing 7352/42

This cluster of small huts survives adjacent to the Control Tower.
They are believed to have been workshops.

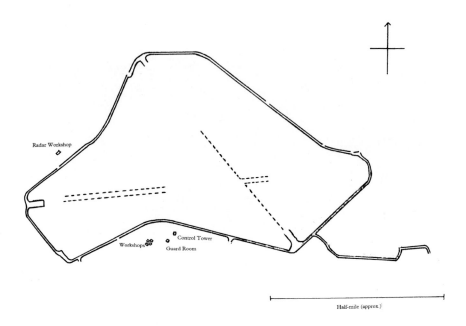

Radar Workshop

Workshops
Control Tower
Guard Room

Half-mile (approx.)

LEISTON

The ghostly ruins of the former Communal Site dispersed just south of Leiston airfield. The remains of at least seven buildings can be found at this location.

They were known as the 'Yoxford Boys'. From January 1944 to the end of the War in Europe the 357th Fighter Group – flying the incomparable P51 Mustang – cut a devastating swathe through the fighter defences of Nazi Germany, paving the way for 8thAF bombers to do their destructive work. Over 313 missions they accounted for 609 enemy aircraft destroyed, either in air-to-air combat or ground attacks; among their pilots were some 40 'aces', including one of the greatest flyers of all time.

And yet it might have been so very different, for the Mustang was initially earmarked for the 9th Air Force, while the first occupants of the airfield at Leiston, in November 1943, were the 358th FG, flying the P47 Thunderbolt. While still formidable, the 'Jug' was no longer an ideal escort fighter, and 8thAF command was anxious to acquire the much more promising P51. The novel solution was a straightforward swap of fighter units between the two air forces, meaning the 358th relocated to Raydon to clear the way for the 357th.

Despite early teething troubles – most significantly, sheer lack of the new North American fighters – it didn't take long for the newcomers to establish themselves as a superb fighting unit. By 6th March 1944 they were escorting bombers all the way to Berlin, returning with claims of 20 enemy aircraft for no combat losses. The 357th – and the Mustang – had arrived.

The Berlin mission was followed by another 20-aircraft claim over Leipzig in June, this combined haul producing the 357th's first Distinguished Unit Citation. Their second came after a colossal aerial engagement over Brandenburg, 14th January 1945, when the Group took on a formation of Bf109s and Fw190s estimated at 120 aircraft, claiming no less than 48.

Captain Leonard Carson, with 18.5 victories, was the 357th's highest-scoring pilot, but he was not the most famous. That distinction went to one Charles 'Chuck' Yeager, whose noted antipathy towards England and the English did not prevent him from attaining 'ace-in-a-day' status on 20th October 1944, accounting for five of eight 357th kills that day. Later shot down over France, Yeager evaded capture and with Resistance help made his way back to his unit – the first American fighter pilot to do so. He finished the war with 11.5 victories, but his place in aviation legend was not fully cemented until 14th October 1947, when he flew an experimental Bell X-1 rocket plane named *Glamorous Glennis* through the mythical 'sound barrier', ushering in the era of supersonic flight and, ultimately, the Space Age.

With the 357th's departure to occupied Germany in July 1945, Leiston was briefly retained by the RAF but had been sold off by the mid-1950s. Today, much of this historic site is given over to a caravan park, while the rest is in agricultural use. There are two memorials to the brave warriors of the 357th, the most striking being a large fibreglass replica of their lethal mount, the P51 Mustang.

Operational history
Nov 43 – Jan 44: 358th FG USAAF (P47D Thunderbolt – bomber escort)
Jan 44 – Jul 45: 357th FG USAAF (P51C,B,D Mustang – bomber escort)

Location
NE of Leiston, N of B1119.   Harrow Lane bisects SW corner of site.

The former Guard Room survives in very good condition in agricultural use.

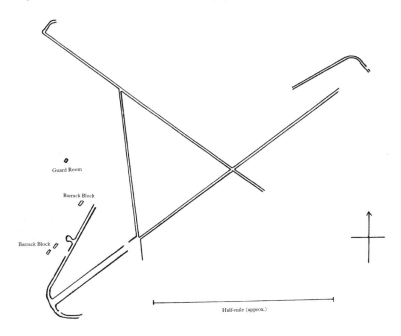

A view south along one of Leiston's few surviving fragments of runway.

This heavily overgrown Picket Post once controlled access to Site no. 9.

MARTLESHAM HEATH

Main Gate sign from Martlesham now preserved at Flixton. The 'Heathens'
were a USAF communications unit, based at the site in its latter years.

Few airfield sites in Great Britain can lay claim to as rich a history as
Martlesham Heath. It opened in January 1917 under Royal Flying Corps
auspices, and immediately became home to the Aeroplane Experimental
Unit, tasked with the evaluation of new aircraft types along with captured
enemy machines. This role would continue, under RAF control, right up
until the outbreak of WW2. In 1924 the operation was renamed the
Aircraft & Armament Experimental Establishment, expanding its remit to
weapons evaluation and now including civilian types in the dizzying array
of prototypes to fly from its runways.

Somewhat surprisingly, given the largely secret nature of its work,
Martlesham was pre-war a major air-show venue, hosting an Empire Air
Day on 25th May 1936, and again just a few months before the onset of
hostilities, 20th May 1939. The tensions of the late thirties saw a hectic
build-up of activities, with testing of new bomber and fighter types, some of
which would go on to become combat legends, while others would
disappear without trace. One particularly notable resident in May 1936 was
an attractive little fighter from the Supermarine stable, carrying the RAF
serial K5054: it was of a type originally to have been known as the Shrew,
but went on to be called by a name that today has a certain resonance –
Spitfire.

Expansion-era Station Headquarters at Martlesham.

The outbreak of war in September 1939 saw the A&AEE relocate to Boscombe Down in Wiltshire, and signalled a major change of role for Martlesham. 11 Group, Fighter Command, took control of the field, which would go on to play a key role in the Battle of Britain, and by late 1939 two major RAF fighter types were in residence. The first was the Hawker Hurricane, culmination of a long line of supremely elegant fighters from the drawing board of Sir Sydney Camm. The Hurricane became the workhorse of the Battle of Britain, accounting for more enemy aircraft than all other fighters and ground defences combined. Though never as revered as the Spitfire, it nonetheless earned its place in aviation legend.

The same cannot be said for the Boulton-Paul Defiant, which today is largely forgotten. This curious fighter was equipped with a gun turret, mounted mid-fuselage, in place of the more conventional armament in the wings. The weight of this turret, not to mention the second crewman required to operate it, severely compromised the Defiant's manoeuvrability, and despite some spectacular early successes against Luftwaffe fighters (who mistook it for the Hurricane), it was outclassed in a matter of weeks. Ultimately relegated to night fighting, the Defiant was another example of a design concept found badly wanting in the heat of actual combat.

Martlesham was heavily involved in one of the least recorded aspects of the Battle of Britain: the sporadic raids by Italy's Regia Aeronautica. Flying patently obsolescent bombers and fighters the Italians were no match for the RAF, and the results speak for themselves – on 11th November 1940 eight out of ten BR20 bombers, plus four fighter escorts, were dispatched for no loss.

This rare type A hangar survives in industrial use. The type A was the standard RAF hangar of the 1920s.

Late in 1943 Martlesham underwent a major upgrade, in preparation for the arrival of the Americans. In truth they had already arrived, for among the Heath's Hurricane units had been one of the famous 'Eagle' squadrons, no. 71. But the new occupants were to be a full-fledged USAAF Fighter Group, the 356th. Flying P47s and later P51s, the Group had a chequered career at Martlesham: they accounted for 201 enemy aircraft but suffered 172 losses of their own; the highest loss rate of all 8thAF Fighter Groups. Unusually, the RAF maintained air-sea rescue units at Martlesham all through the 356th's residence, and British fighter types were still to be seen, including the cutting-edge (and highly temperamental) Hawker Typhoon.

With the end of the War, Martlesham Heath returned to its previous existence as a flight-testing centre, hosting even more exotic types than previously, such as the Avro Ashton (an experimental jet airliner pre-dating the DH Comet) and the Short Sperrin (a would-be jet bomber, from the company that produced the Sunderland). Most significant was the Avro 707 delta-winged jet, a precursor of the mighty Vulcan bomber. In 1959, what is today arguably the RAF's most revered unit – the Battle of Britain Memorial Flight – graced the field with its presence.

The onset of the sixties saw Martlesham go into rapid decline, Air Training Corps gliders being the last active residents by 1963. The site was proposed as the future Ipswich Airport, until that status was eventually awarded to Nacton. Today the area is heavily commercialised, most notably by British Telecom, but several buildings survive including the Control Tower, which happily has been restored as a museum, dedicated to preserving the history of this most remarkable airfield.

This former Wireless/Telegraphy Station stands on Foxhall Heath, barely two miles west of Martlesham. It is now the home of the Suffolk Aviation Centre.

Martlesham Heath's restored Watch Office now sits incongruously in the middle of a housing estate.

The various memorials installed at Martlesham are a tribute to the airfield's rich history.

Operational history

Jul 23 – May 34: 22 sqn (DH9A / Horsley – trials)

Mar 24 – May 34: 15 sqn (DH9A / Horsley – trials)

Sep 36 – May 38: 64 sqn (Demon – fighter)

Dec 38 – May 40: 29 sqn* (Blenheim If – night-fighter)

May 39 – Mar 42: 110 sqn*(Blenheim I,IV – light bombing)

Sep 39 – Jan 40:   604 sqn* (Blenheim I – light bombing)

Oct 39 – May 40: 25 sqn* (Blenheim If – night-fighter)

Dec 39 – Apr 40: 17 sqn (Hurricane I – fighter)

Dec 39 – Feb 40: 236 sqn (Blenheim If – night-fighter)

Dec 39 – May 40: 264 sqn (Defiant I – fighter)

Dec 39 – May 40: 504 sqn (Hurricane I – fighter)

Mar 40 – May 40: 266 sqn (Spitfire I – fighter)

May 40:   151 sqn (Hurricane I – fighter)

May 40 – Aug 40: 85 sqn* (Hurricane I – fighter)

Jun 40:   25 sqn (Blenheim If – night-fighter)

Aug 40 – Oct 40: 264 sqn* (Defiant I – fighter)

Sep 40 – Oct 40:   257 sqn (Hurricane I – fighter)

Sep 40 – Jul 41:   613 sqn* (Lysander II,IIIa – coastal patrol/air-sea rescue)

Oct 40:   17 sqn (Hurricane IIa – fighter)

Nov 40 – Dec 40: 257 sqn (Hurricane I – fighter)

Dec 40 – Apr 41: 242 sqn (Hurricane I,IIb – fighter)

Feb 41 – Mar 41: 605 sqn (Hurricane IIa – fighter)

Apr 41 – Jun 41: 3 sqn (Hurricane IIb,IIc – fighter)

May 41:   64 sqn (Spitfire IIa – fighter)

Jun 41 – Jul 41:   402 sqn (Hurricane IIa,IIb – fighter)

Jul 41 – Oct 41:   258 sqn (Hurricane IIa – fighter)

Jul 41 – Aug 41:   312 sqn (Hurricane IIb – fighter)

Aug 41:   54 sqn (Spitfire Vb – fighter)

Aug 41 – Oct 41: 607 sqn (Hurricane IIa,IIb – fighter)

Oct 41 – Dec 41: 403 sqn (Spitfire Vb – fighter)

Nov 41 – Jul 44: 287 sqn* (Blenheim IV / Hudson III / Lysander II /
Hurricane I,IIb,IV / Master III / Defiant I,III / Oxford / Martinet /
Spitfire Vb – target towing/gunnery training)

Dec 41:   2 sqn (Tomahawk I,II – army co-operation)

Dec 41 – May 42: 71 sqn (Spitfire Vb – fighter)

Dec 41 – Oct 44: 277 sqn* (Lysander III / Walrus / Defiant I / Spitfire
IIc,Vb / Sea Otter – air-sea rescue)

82

May 42 – Jun 42: 412 sqn (Spitfire Vb – fighter)
Jun 42:   41 sqn (Spitfire Vb – fighter)
Jun 42:   65 sqn (Spitfire Vb – fighter)
Jun 42 – Jul 42: 122 sqn (Spitfire Vb – fighter)
Jun 42:   403 sqn (Spitfire Vb – fighter)
Jul 42:   124 sqn (Spitfire Vb – fighter)
Jul 42:   350 sqn (Spitfire Vb – fighter)
Jul 42 – Aug 42: 401 sqn (Spitfire IX – fighter)
Jul 42 – Nov 42: 416 sqn (Spitfire Vb – fighter)
Jul 42:   611 sqn (Spitfire Vb – fighter)
Aug 42:   133 sqn (Spitfire Vb – fighter)
Aug 42 – Nov 42 165 sqn* (Spitfire Vb – fighter)
Aug 42 – Dec 42: 182 sqn (Hurricane I / Typhoon Ia,IIb – fighter)
Sep 42:   111 sqn (Spitfire Vb – fighter)
Sep 42:   132 sqn (Spitfire Vb – fighter)
Sep 42:   332 sqn (Spitfire Vb – fighter)
Sep 42:   350 sqn (Spitfire Vb – fighter)
Oct 42 – Feb 43: 132 sqn (Spitfire Vb – fighter)
Nov 42 – Dec 42: 453 sqn (Spitfire Vb – fighter)
Feb 43:   132 sqn (Spitfire Vb – fighter)
Mar 43 – Apr 43: 303 sqn (Spitfire Vb – fighter)
Apr 43:   222 sqn (Spitfire Vb – fighter)
Apr 43 – Jun 43: 317 sqn (Spitfire Vb – fighter)
Apr 43:   421 sqn (Spitfire Vb – fighter)
May 43 – Jun 43: 284 sqn (Walrus – air-sea rescue)
May 43 – Jun 43: 501 sqn (Spitfire Vb – fighter)
Jun 43 – Aug 43: 198 sqn (Typhoon Ib – fighter)
Jun 43 – Jul 43: 239 sqn (Mustang I – army co-operation)
Jul 43:   26 sqn (Mustang I – ground attack)
Jul 43:   401 sqn (Spitfire Vb – fighter)
Oct 43 – May 45: 356th FG USAAF (P47D Thunderbolt / P51D Mustang
– bomber escort)
Feb 44 – Apr 44: 1 sqn (Typhoon Ib – fighter)
Sep 44 – Feb 45: 278 sqn (Warwick I / Spitfire Vb / Walrus – air-sea
rescue)
Jun 55 – Jun 56: 22 sqn* (Sycamore HC12 / Whirlwind HAR2 – air-sea
rescue)
*Denotes detachment only

NOTE: 15 & 22 were the nominal squadrons of the A&AEE – aircraft assets listed were in case of operational activation.

Location

S of Martlesham, E of Kesgrave. The A12 bisects the site, running N-S.

The former Guard Room, with the surviving hangar visible beyond.

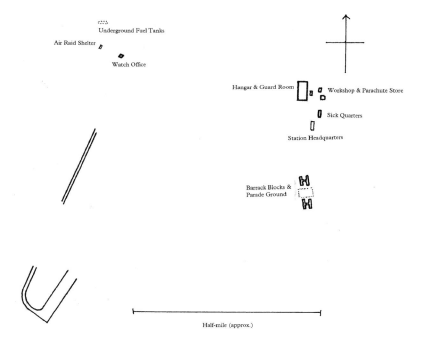

So-called 'half-H' Barrack Blocks to drawing 444/36, with the Parade Square in the foreground.

Underground Fuel Stores preserved at Martlesham.

MENDLESHAM

The view east along a portion of the former E-W runway.

Today a section of runway and a handful of buildings are virtually all that remain of Mendlesham airfield. But the site is impossible to miss, thanks to the looming presence of a TV transmission mast, which has become a prominent local landmark. The airfield was not completed until late in 1943, and, though earmarked for the USAAF, its initial occupants were RAF squadrons, flying the definitive RAF aircraft – the Spitfire.

Squadrons 310, 312 & 313 were Czech units, 310 in particular already boasting a storied history. Originally formed at Duxford in 1940 with Hurricanes, they had fought with distinction as part of Douglas Bader's 'Big Wing' during the Battle of Britain. Now they boasted Mk IX Spitfires, the most widely produced and arguably most successful version of the classic fighter.

The Spitfire is, quite simply, a legend, the most famous military aircraft of all time and, along with Concorde, the most easily recognisable shape in the sky. Fast, nimble, and a positive delight to fly, the 'Spit' leapt from Reginald Mitchell's drawing board into immortality, evolving through 21 major marks as it remained in production right through the War, along with its two superb Rolls-Royce engines, the Merlin and the Griffon. Mendlesham's Czech Mk IXs were primarily tasked with so-called 'Ramrod' missions, escorting medium bombers on daylight tactical raids.

In April 1944 the familiar shapes of B24 Liberators arrived at Mendlesham, flown by the USAAF 34th Bomb Group. The 34th was the oldest Bomb Group to join the 8thAF, having been activated on 15th January 1941 at Langley Field, Virginia. They commenced operations on 23rd May 1944, and flew 62 missions with B24s before switching to B17 Fortresses in September. Most of their early targets were tactical in nature as they supported the build-up to D-Day, but they eventually progressed to strategic bombing. Throughout, the 34th had an exemplary low loss rate, losing just 34 aircraft in combat, none of them to enemy fighters. To put this in perspective, the Group actually suffered more losses – 39 – to accidents than they did to enemy action!

The 34th departed Mendlesham in July 1945, after which the site was used as a surplus ammunition store until final closure in June 1954. Creeping industrialisation steadily fragmented the site, but in the shadow of the TV mast could be found an extraordinary memorial to the 34th BG – a bronze relief of a bomber pilot, sculpted by Baltimore artist Henry Berg. This at least was the case until 2010, when, disgustingly, the installation was vandalised for its metal elements – it is to be fervently hoped that a replacement can be fashioned as soon as possible.

Remains of a dispersed site on the northern edge of Mendlesham, believed to have been the Hospital complex. The small tower on the building at the left denotes an Ablutions Block

87

Operational history

Feb 44 – Mar 44: 310 sqn (Spitfire Vb, LfIXb – bomber escort)
Mar 44 – Apr 44: 312 sqn (Spitfire Vb, LfIXb – bomber escort)
Mar 44 – Apr 44: 313 sqn (Spitfire Vb, LfIXb – bomber escort)
Apr 44 – Aug 45: 34th BG USAAF (B24H,J Liberator, B17G Flying
Fortress heavy bombing)

Location

SE of Mendlesham, E of A140. Town Lane passes N of the site,
intersecting the former NE-SW runway

A poignant message of gratitude left at the now vandalised memorial site.
The inscription reads:

'Thank you for your sacrifice. You helped destroy the evil axis
regimes of hate. Without your bravery and many men like you,
Germany would have taken all Europe including us. We owe you a
great debt. It is with our eternal gratitude and respect we
thank you.
You will always have a place in our hearts and a part of England
will always be yours.

A Standby Set House. These buildings contained diesel generators for emergency power – their durability and usefulness have ensured that a large number have survived until the present day.

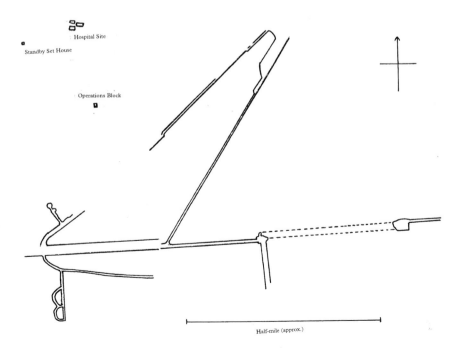

Hospital Site

Standby Set House

Operations Block

Half-mile (approx.)

METFIELD

The Braithwaite High-Level Water Tank is one of the classic airfield structures. Metfield's is a particularly fine example.

Metfield had an operational life of less than two years, yet it managed to feature the three major components of the USAAF – bombers, fighters and transports. The fighters were, almost inevitably, P47 Thunderbolts, and they belonged to the 353rd FG, who in August 1943 moved in from Goxhill in Lincolnshire. They began with the standard bomber escort missions, but soon moved on to more offensive missions such as dive-bombing and low-level strafing of tactical targets, especially airfields. With the invasion of Occupied Europe on the horizon, the 353rd relocated to Raydon in April 1944.

In place of heavy fighters came heavy bombers – the B24 Liberators of the 491st BG, aka 'The Ringmasters'. They commenced operations on 2nd June, tactical raids with D-Day looming. The 491st would eventually go on to compile more missions than any other 8thAF B24 Group, but their campaign was not without blemish: on the 24th and 25th July, in support of the St Lo breakout, they twice accidentally bombed Allied lines. Earlier, on 15th July, Metfield itself suffered an unfortunate reverse when the Bomb Dump blew up, causing loss of life and a four-day suspension of operations. A subsequent investigation decided that the explosion had been accidentally caused.

In August the 491st moved on to North Pickenham in Norfolk, replacing the unfortunate 492nd BG who had been effectively wiped out in a short and disastrous campaign. This cleared Metfield for the arrival of American transport aircraft, an unusual sight in wartime Suffolk. Chief among these was, of course, the Douglas C47 Skytrain, perhaps better known by its civilian designation, DC-3, and its RAF name – Dakota. Originating as an airliner in the mid-thirties, the C47 not only boasted exceptionally good looks, but its method of construction made it virtually impervious to airframe fatigue. Indeed, the Dakota remains a highly active transport to this day, although its passenger-carrying operation in Europe was recently disrupted by woefully misguided EU legislation; however, the situation is improving.

Along with C47s there were also mighty C54 Skymasters and transport versions of the Liberator. These latter undertook some of the most unusual operations of the War – clandestine flights to neutral Sweden to look after the interests of the many US aircraft and airmen that had been interned there. Though the vast majority of bombers had been forced down by heavy damage or mechanical failures, there was a suspicion that at least some had opted to land in Sweden as an escape from the long odds of surviving a full operational tour.

At War's end Metfield was handed over to the RAF, but they had no use for it and by the end of 1945, the site was abandoned. Even so, over sixty years on, substantial sections of the runways remain, along with a handful of buildings, albeit in poor condition. A memorial has fairly recently been installed, to remind passers-by of the surprisingly rich history of this out-of-the-way location.

Operational history
Aug 43 – Apr 44: 353rd FG USAAF (P47D Thunderbolt – bomber escort / ground attack)
Apr 44 – Aug 44: 491st BG USAAF (B24H Liberator – heavy bombing)
Aug 44 – May 45: 1409th Base Unit USAAF (B24/C87 Liberator, C47 Skytrain, C54 Skymaster – transport / special ops)

Location
E of Metfield, E of B1123. Christmas Lane bisects site.

A view west across the airfield, along part of the former E-W runway.

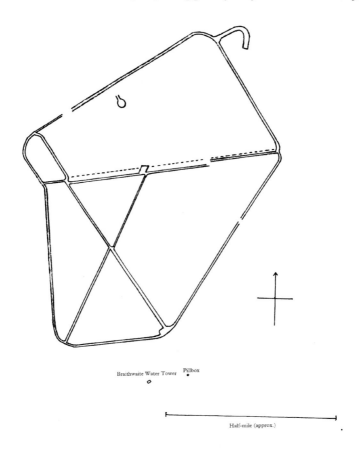

Braithwaite Water Tower   Pillbox

Half-mile (approx.)

NEWMARKET HEATH

Rare survivor, a type B1 hangar on the north side of the current A14 trunk road. In the foreground is one of the very few substantial portions of taxiway remaining at the Newmarket site.

Newmarket Heath is, of course, indelibly associated with horse racing, which has occurred at the site since at least the 12th century under royal auspices, hence the 'Sport of Kings'. But Newmarket also has a long-standing, though less well known, association with aviation. It was first used as a landing ground in WW1, and from the 1920s private aircraft graced the area on race days, a situation that continues to this day. In 1938, with war once again brewing, the Air Ministry resumed its interest, and Newmarket Heath became a satellite to Mildenhall.

99 sqn took up residence just as the new conflict broke out, flying the aircraft that was to be the mainstay of Bomber Command in the early years of WW2 – the Vickers Wellington. The 'Wimpey', as it was affectionately known, dated back to 1936, and owed its unique 'geodetic' construction to the genius of Barnes Wallis, who also fathered the Bouncing Bomb. The result was a bomber that, although not blessed with great performance, was extremely durable, and it went on to be produced in remarkable numbers, with over 11,000 eventually being built.

Like so many Wellington squadrons, 99 bore the brunt of Bomber Command's early, disastrous daylight operations. One such, on 14th December 1939, saw five of twelve aircraft shot down during a raid on warships off Heligoland: two more collided in mid-air, and an eighth crashed en route back to Newmarket. This mission is cited as being the final straw that led to Bomber Command switching to night operations.

In February 1941 four-engine 'heavies' appeared at Newmarket, in the form of 7 sqn's Stirlings. In the spring, control of the field switched to Stradishall, and even more unusual types arrived courtesy of 138 & 161 sqns, Special Operations units that supported SOE activities. Mainstay of Special Ops was the bizarre Westland Lysander, an unsuccessful Army co-operation design that found a new niche, and lasting fame, dropping and collecting secret agents in occupied France. In addition, both squadrons operated obsolescent Armstrong-Whitworth Whitley bombers and 138 flew a single American Martin Maryland on its clandestine missions.

Newmarket may seem a curiously public location from which to operate an essentially secret unit, but other hush-hush activities were undertaken during 1942. The Heath's vast runway space was considered ideal for testing the little-known General Aircraft Hamilcar, a tank-carrying glider. Later came a most significant aircraft, the Gloster F9/40 powered by Frank Whittle's ground-breaking jet engine. This tiny, underpowered machine was a glimpse of the future of air warfare for those lucky, and clever enough to see it.

By September 1943 another largely secret operation, the Bombing Development Unit, had arrived to trial an assortment of new bombing aids. They remained until 1945, along with various training units, but Newmarket's days as a military airfield were numbered. Flying ceased in February of that year, and by the summer the RAF had abandoned the site for good. Today it is left to the engines of light aircraft to distract from the continual drum of hoof-beats, and remind onlookers of Newmarket's 'other' history.

Operational history

May 39 – Mar 41: 107 sqn* (Blenheim IV – light bombing)
Sep 39 – Mar 40: 99 sqn (Wellington I,Ia – bombing)
Aug 41:   138sqn* (Lysander IIIa / Whitley IV / Maryland – special ops)
Dec 41 – Jan 42: 215 sqn (Wellington Ia – bombing)

Feb 42 – Mar 42: 161 sqn (Lysander IIIa / Hudson I / Whitley V – special ops)
Nov 42 – Jun 43: 75 sqn (Stirling I,III – heavy bombing)
Jan 43 – Mar 43: 2 sqn* (Mustang I – army co-operation)
Mar 43:   453 sqn (Spitfire Vb – fighter)

NOTES: 138 sqn was originally 1419 Flt; part of this squadron was merged with the King's Flight to form 161sqn.

*indicates detachment only

Location
Newmarket Heath, E of A14. Exercise tracks N of main course occupy airfield site. Surviving buildings are on opposite (W) side of A14.

Among the tiny handful of buildings still extant at Newmarket is this Latrine Block – a vital but unappreciated part of airfield infrastructure.

RATTLESDEN

The magnificent full-width surviving section of Rattlesden's NE-SW runway.
The present-day glider complex is upper right, with the Control Tower just visible
next to the small blister-style hangar.

The airfield at Rattlesden was constructed in 1942, and on completion handed over to the USAAF. In December, elements of the 322nd BG took up residence and remained until April 1943, when they and their B26 Marauder aircraft were relocated to Rougham.

Not until November 1943 did the site become home to the unit with which it would become synonymous – the B17-equipped 447th Bomb Group. During their time at Rattlesden the 447th undertook 256 missions, suffering 97 combat losses and a further 43 to accidents. Their worst days were 25th April 1944, when they lost ten Fortresses shot down and another forced to ditch during a raid on Berlin; and 2nd November 1944, when five aircraft were lost on a mission to Merseburg. It was during this latter operation that 2nd Lt. Robert Femoyer earned the Medal of Honour, sadly to be awarded posthumously. The bomber on which Femoyer was navigator sustained several shrapnel hits, but despite being severely wounded he refused immediate treatment and remained at his post, guiding the pilots around known flak emplacements and towards safety. Not until his aircraft was over the North Sea did Femoyer allow himself to at least be sedated with morphine: his crew made it back to Rattlesden, but Femoyer succumbed to his injuries shortly after.

Despite these brutal reverses, the 447th established a reputation for bombing accuracy that was among the highest in the 8thAF. Several of their aircraft put together phenomenal combat records: *Milk Wagon* racked up 127 missions, while *Scheherazade* also broke the 100-mission mark. However, the most celebrated Fortress to fly for the 447th belonged to its 709th squadron, carried the serial 42-97976 and the name, *A Bit o' Lace*.

There could be no mistaking *A Bit o' Lace* at Rattlesden, or anywhere else. Stretched along the entire nose was a voluptuous rendition of the notorious comic strip character 'Miss Lace'. The artwork was painted by the 447th's resident nose artist, Nick Fingelly, based on an original sketch by Miss Lace's creator, famed cartoonist Milton Caniff. Indeed, such was Fingelly's attention to detail that he even reproduced Caniff's unmistakable 'box' signature – a selfless move that was to cause confusion to some post-war researchers who deduced, quite wrongly, that Caniff himself had painted the aircraft.

Following delivery in March 1944, *Lace* survived over eighty gruelling combat missions, including one to Kiel on 4th April 1945, when a direct flak hit tore away a huge chunk of her tail. After VE Day she participated in victory flypasts and then began the long trip back to the States where, like so many Fortresses, she ended her days at the huge scrapyard in Kingman, Arizona. However, *Lace* was to gain immortality, and enter the lives of generations of schoolboys, when in 1962 she became subject of the ground-breaking Airfix 1:72nd scale B17 plastic model kit, in production for over 30 years and still highly sought after today.

In October 1945 Rattlesden was returned to the RAF, and in the immediate post-war period became a supply depot for the Ministry of Food, and later an emergency landing ground for Wattisham. In the early sixties the site became a launch pad for Bloodhound surface-to-air missiles. Today a healthy number of buildings survive, and happily aviation still has a part to play: since 1976 the runways and former Control Tower have played host to the Rattlesden Gliding Club, whose elegant flying machines and attendant towing aircraft keep the spirit of this fine field alive.

Location
SE of Felsham – minor road running south from village crosses surviving runway.

Operational history

Nov 43 – Aug 45: 447th BG USAAF (B17G Flying Fortress – heavy bombing)

Dec 59 – Jun 64: 266sqn (Bloodhound I – missile defence

Rattlesden's later years are represented by this building, part of the Bloodhound Maintenance Unit. It is in a surprisingly advanced state of dilapidation.

Another reminder of the 447th's time at Rattlesden is the striking weathervane.

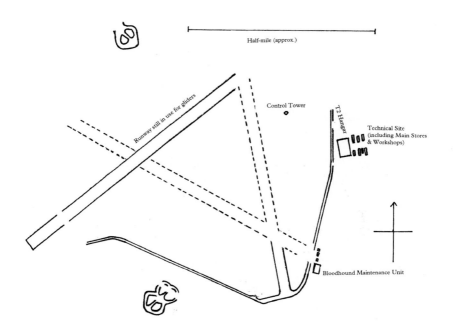

Half-mile (approx.)

Runway still in use for gliders

Control Tower

T2 Hangar

Technical Site
(including Main Stores
& Workshops)

Bloodhound Maintenance Unit

RAYDON

Viewed from the right angle, Raydon is still very much an airfield. This view looking west shows part of the N-S runway in the foreground, with a T2 hangar beyond and a pair of Romney huts. The Perimeter Track can just be glimpsed at the extreme right.

The 'swapping' of fighter units between the 8th and 9th Air Forces of the USAAF, with the primary aim of obtaining P51 Mustangs for the 'Mighty Eighth', has already been described in this volume. It was responsible for the shuttling of Groups in and out of Raydon – originally intended as a bomber airfield when construction began in 1942 - from late 1943 to the spring of 1944. There was indeed a marked contrast between the brutish P47 and the state-of-the-art P51, a difference fully experienced by the unit that was to become Raydon's major resident: the 353rd FG.

Somewhat ironically, the 353rd was the last 8th AF Fighter Group to transition from the Thunderbolt to the Mustang, not completing this change until October 1944. The Group had a lot of faith in the 'Jug'; flying it, they had claimed 21 enemy aircraft on 8th May and earned a Distinguished Unit Citation for operations in September in support of the ill-fated Operation Market Garden. On the debit side, they had suffered eight losses on 12th May during an attack on the Pas de Calais.

With the incomparable P51, the 353rd went on to even greater successes. November 28th saw 18 aircraft claimed, while on 24th March

1945 the tally was 23, with two pilots attaining 'ace-in-a-day' status. The climax came on 16th April when, as part of a mass attack on enemy airfields, the Group accounted for 128 aircraft destroyed on the ground, plus a further three air-to-air kills. The final tally for the Group was an astonishing 330 aircraft shot down and in excess of 400 obliterated on the ground – they had produced no less than 17 aces in the process.

The Americans lingered at Raydon after the war, in the form of the 652nd Weather Squadron who remained until December 1945. Handed over to the RAF, the airfield was formally disposed of in 1958. Today a pair of T2 hangars remain along with several other buildings, as well as substantial sections of runway and perimeter track – these latter have enabled occasional air shows to be staged in recent years, with preserved 'warbirds' evoking the wartime spirit of the site. There is also a most impressive permanent memorial to the Americans who gave their all in the liberation of Europe, and they are further commemorated in Raydon church.

Crew Lockers and Drying Rooms at Raydon. Airmen's flight suits could be by turns subjected to ice and copious amounts of sweat, thus requiring careful handling and storage.

Location
NE of Raydon, W of Wenham Magna, E of B1123. Woodlands Road bisects western portion of site.

101

*The breath-taking memorial at Raydon occupies what remains
of the E-W runway.*

Operational history

Dec 43 – Jan 44: 357th FG USAAF (P51C Mustang – bomber escort)

Feb 44 – Apr 44: 358th FG USAAF (P47D Thunderbolt – bomber escort)

Apr 44 – Oct 45: 353rd FG USAAF (P47D Thunderbolt / P51D,K Mustang – bomber escort)

Oct 45 – Dec 45: 652nd WS USAAF (B24 Liberator – weather reconnaissance)

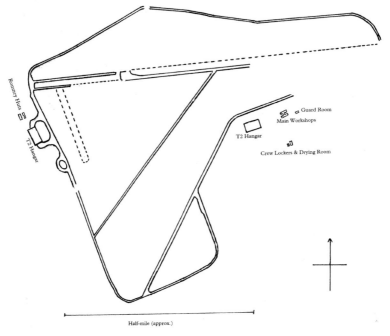

SHEPHERD'S GROVE

A large number of Technical Site buildings survive in industrial usage. Shown here are the Main Stores, consisting of two Romney huts flanking a central office, and beyond, the Parachute Store with its distinctive hanging tower.

As has been noted, the naming of military airfields during the hectic phase of aerodrome construction in WW2 was cause for frequent confusion. Airfields were regularly known locally by an entirely different name from the official designation, and some actually changed names during the course of the conflict. Ostensibly the policy was to name an airfield after the nearest town or village, but as new sites proliferated it was also vital not to have too many similar-sounding names, in order to avoid misunderstandings, especially in the realms of radio communication and telephony. The name Shepherd's Grove evokes a particularly bucolic image, and indeed the airfield was unusual in that it was named not for a community, but for a nearby wood.

Shepherd's Grove came late to the party, not becoming operational until April 1944. It had been intended for American bombers but was not, in the event, required, becoming instead a satellite to Stradishall. In a rather ironic twist, this seemingly superfluous station would go on to become a major American base in the Cold War era.

The aircraft that defined Shepherd's Grove during its brief wartime career was the much-maligned Stirling. In the closing months of the conflict 196 and 299 sqns – operating the Mk IV transport version –

provided vital support to SOE operations and also towed assault gliders participating in the Rhineland crossing. The Stirlings remained until spring 1946, after which Shepherd's Grove came under the control of Watton, seeing numerous aircraft of the Radio Warfare Establishment, especially Ansons and Lancasters.

The RAF relinquished control of the airfield in 1950, and it was transferred to the now independent United States Air Force. August 1951 saw the arrival of the 81st Fighter Interceptor Wing, flying the matchless F86A Sabre. Emerging from the same North American stable as the Mustang, the Sabre was arguably the finest of the early jet fighters, racking up an astonishing kill ratio in the Korean War. The presence of the 81st FIW in Suffolk had historical significance, as it became the first foreign unit assigned to the air defence of the United Kingdom. The 81st was later augmented by the pugnacious Republic F84F Thunderstreak, a jet descendent of the mighty P47. In 1958 the 81st relocated to Woodbridge, and it would remain an integral part of Suffolk skies for over forty years.

Shepherd's Grove saw out its military service signifying the Cold War at its most chilling, becoming a base for the Thor nuclear missiles of 82sqn. Thankfully, the Thors were never called upon to do their apocalyptic work, and with their removal in 1963 the airfield's operational life came to a close. Today the runways and taxiways are long gone, however much of the Technical Site still survives within an industrial estate, offering an intriguing glimpse of a largely forgotten, yet highly significant, part of military history.

The site at Shepherd's Grove is heavily fragmented. This building survives in splendid isolation on the eastern side of the former airfield, and is believed to have been the Station Armoury.

Operational history

Apr 44 – Oct 44: 1657 HCU (Stirling – bomber training)
Jan 45 – Mar 46: 196 sqn (Stirling IV – transport)
Jan 45 – Feb 45: 299 sqn (Stirling IV – transport)
Jan 45 – Apr 45: 1677 TTF (Martinet TT.1 – target-towing)
Aug 51 – Dec 58: 81st FIW USAF (F86A Sabre / F84F Thunderstreak – air defence)
Jul 59 – Dec 63:   82 sqn (Thor IRBM – nuclear deterrent/strike)

Location

E of Stanton, S of A143. Grove Lane & Upthorpe Road connect to airfield site.

The former Gymnasium, with a chancel extension (right), to drawing 14604/40. Gyms were frequently co-opted as chapels, not to mention cinemas, impromptu briefing rooms and dance halls. Later it became the Base Exchange.

The northern edge of Shepherd's Grove has reverted to agriculture. The cluster of Nissen-type huts in the distance formed the Officers' Mess in WW2, and became a social club during the airfield's Cold War career.

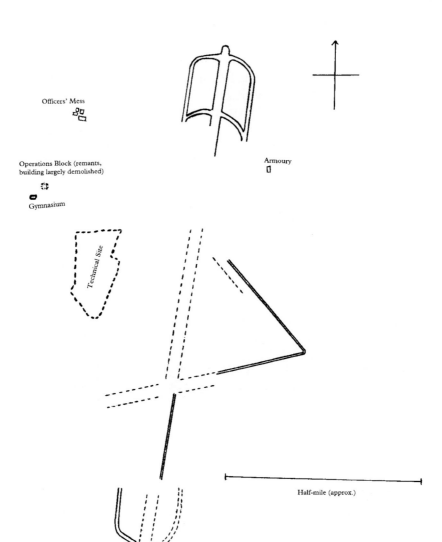

Officers' Mess

Operations Block (remants,
building largely demolished)

Gymnasium

Armoury

Technical Site

Half-mile (approx.)

STRADISHALL

The beautifully preserved Officers' Mess,
to the classic expansion era drawing 570/38.

The military airfields of WW2 have suffered a variety of fates in the modern era. The vast majority have simply returned to the agricultural land from which they were first fashioned, albeit frequently with an attendant industrial concern to make use of the durable buildings and concrete hard standings. Few, however, have suffered quite so ignominiously as Stradishall, which in July 1977 became Highpoint Prison. This is especially galling given Stradishall's remarkably rich history, which encompasses an extraordinary variety of squadrons and aircraft types, in particular a long association with Bomber Command and its most famous instrument of destruction, the Avro Lancaster.

Stradishall was an Expansion-era airfield, opening in February 1938 and being home initially to 9 & 148 sqns, flying such primitive types as the Handley-Page Heyford biplane bomber and the ungainly Vickers Wellesley. By the eve of war both squadrons had converted to the rather more modern Wellington, and been joined by 75 sqn.

It is somewhat surprising to note that Stradishall actually closed to flying in September 1939, re-opening in October as a temporary home for 236 & 254 sqns, flying the night-fighter version of the Bristol Blenheim. By early 1940 the airfield had reverted to a bomber base, seeing a wide array of squadrons and types as Bomber Command struggled to adjust to the verities of armed conflict with its frequently outclassed and outdated machines.

214 sqn were resident longest, remaining until the autumn of 1942. Equipped initially with Wellingtons, they had a tough time of it, losing seven of fourteen aircraft on the night of 1st-2nd April 1942 during a low-level attack on railway targets at Hanau and Lohr. Previously, they had participated in bizarre fire-raising missions, which involved dropping incendiaries on forested areas and harvest fields in southern Germany – arguably the most pointless bombing operations of the entire War. Converting to Stirlings, 214 took part in the first 1,000-bomber raid on Cologne, which signalled Bomber Command's resurgence and a turning point in the European air war.

In December 1944 the Lancaster finally made its appearance at Stradishall. A prime example of success salvaged from disaster, the Lancaster evolved from the ill-fated Manchester, a twin-engine type fatally undermined by the unreliability of its Roll-Royce Vulture powerplants. Avro designer Roy Chadwick kept the best elements of the Manchester, crafting a new, larger bomber propelled by four Merlins – the finest aero engines available. The result was a world-class machine capable of carrying preposterously heavy bomb loads, up to and including the monstrous 22,000lb *Grand Slam*. The Lancaster III, as operated by 186 sqn, remained at Stradishall until after the close of hostilities.

The immediate post-war period saw four-engine 'heavies' remain a feature at Stradishall. Initially these were benign transport types, mainly Stirlings but also the Avro York, which was based directly upon the Lancaster. Then in summer 1946 the 'Lancs' themselves returned, and would remain until 1949 when Stradishall underwent a dramatic change of role.

From September 1949 the site became home to 203 Advanced Flying School, which operated an astonishing mixture of types ranging from the humble Tiger Moth to De Havilland Vampire jets. 203 AFS was subsequently re-designated 226 Operational Conversion Unit and remained until June 1955.

Now the focus shifted again, and Stradishall became a full-blown fighter station. Among the types operated was the mighty delta-winged Gloster Javelin, but as the fifties merged into the sixties the classically elegant shape of the Hawker Hunter took centre stage. Sadly, the sixties also saw the beginning of Stradishall's decline. In December 1961 it passed to Training Command and for nine years was home to 1 Air Navigation School, before flying activities ceased in August 1970. Interestingly, among the types operated by 1 ANS was the Vickers Varsity, a bulbous descendent of both the Wellesley and the Wellington.

Stradishall made news again in 1977 when it became a transit camp for Ugandan Asians displaced by the hideous Amin regime, just before conversion into a prison complex. Today, many of the former RAF buildings lie hidden behind maximum-security fencing, a grim outcome for one of Suffolk's most redoubtable airfields.

The imposing expansion-era Water Tower now services the prison site.

Operational history
Mar 38 – Jul 39: 9 sqn (Heyford III / Wellington I – bomber)
Mar 38 – Sep 39: 148 sqn (Wellesley / Heyford III / Wellington I / Anson I - bomber)
Jul 39 – Sep 39: 75 sqn (Wellington I / Anson I – bomber)
Oct 39 – Dec 39: 254 sqn (Blenheim If – night-fighter)
Oct 39 – Dec 39: 236 sqn (Blenheim If – night-fighter)

109

Feb 40 – Jan 42: 214 sqn (Wellington Ia,Ic,II – bomber)
Apr 40 – May 40: 148 sqn (Wellington Ic – bomber)
Jun 40 – Jul 40: 150 sqn (Battle – light day bomber)
Sep 40 – Apr 42: 311 sqn* (Wellington Ic – bomber)
Dec 41 – Mar 42: 138 sqn (Whitley V / Lysander IIIa / Halifax II – special ops)
Jan 42 – Oct 42: 214 sqn (Wellington Ic / Stirling I – bomber)
Jan 42 – Mar 42: 215 sqn (Wellington Ic – bomber)
Apr 42 – Aug 42: 109 sqn (Wellington Ic,VI / Anson I – bomber)
Aug 42 – Sep 42: 101 sqn (Wellington III – bomber)
Oct 42 – Dec 44: 1657 HCU (Stirling I / Oxford – bomber training)
Dec 44 – Jul 45: 186 sqn (Lancaster I,III – heavy bomber)
Aug 45 – Aug 46: 51 sqn (Stirling IV,V / York C.1 – transport)
Aug 45 – Dec 45: 158 sqn (Stirling IV,V – transport)
Sep 46 – Feb 49: 35 sqn (Lancaster I,III – heavy bomber)
Sep 46 – Feb 49: 115 sqn (Lancaster B.1 – heavy bomber)
Nov 46 – Feb 49: 149 sqn (Lancaster I,III – heavy bomber)
Nov 46 – Feb 49: 207 sqn (Lancaster I,III – heavy bomber)
Sep 49 – Jun 55: 226 OCU *nee* 203 AFS (Meteor 4,7,8,PR9 / Spitfire 14,16,18 / Vampire 5, T.11 / Harvard / Tempest 5 / Beaufighter TT.10 / Martinet / Oxford / Balliol / Tiger Moth / Mosquito T.3 – training)
Mar 55 – May 57: 125 sqn (Meteor NF.11 / Venom NF.3 – night-fighter)
Jun 55 – Jun 57: 245 sqn (Meteor F.8 / Hunter F.4 – fighter)
Dec 55 – Nov 58: 89 sqn (Javelin FAW.2,FAW.6 / Venom NF.3 – night-fighter)
Jan 57 – Aug 57: 152 sqn (Meteor NF.12,NF.14 – night-fighter)
Aug 57 – Jul 58: 263 sqn (Hunter F.6 – fighter)
Jul 58 – Nov 61: 1 sqn (Hunter F.6,FGA.9 - fighter/strike)
Nov 58 – Jun 59: 85 sqn (Javelin FAW.2,FAW.6 – interceptor)
Jul 59 – Nov 61: 54 sqn (Hunter F.6,FGA.9 – fighter/strike)
Mar 60 – Jun 60: 208 sqn (Hunter FGA.9 – strike)
Jul 60 – Sep 60: 111 sqn (Hunter FGA.9 – strike)
Sep 60 – Oct 60: 43 sqn (Hunter FGA.9 – strike)
Dec 61 – Aug 70: 1 ANS (Varsity / Meteor 7,14 / Dominie T.1 – training)
*Detachment only

Location

SW of Stradishall.   A143 bisects former Accommodation/Technical sites (now prison)

Elegant former Officers' Married Quarters at Stradishall, to drawing 528/539

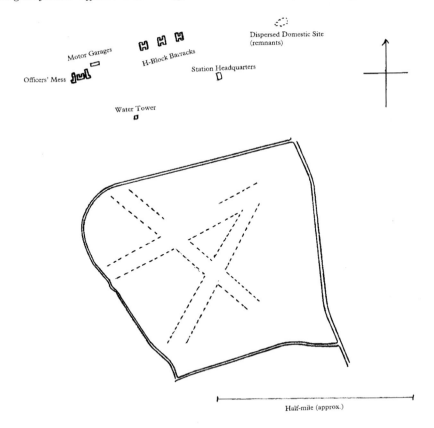

Motor Garages

Officers' Mess

H-Block Barracks

Dispersed Domestic Site
(remnants)

Station Headquarters

Water Tower

Half-mile (approx.)

SUDBURY

A view south-west along the former NE-SW runway, now a public footpath.

Work on the airfield that was eventually named Sudbury began in 1942, but it would not be until March 1944 that it became operational, with the arrival of the USAAF 486th Bomb Group. They would remain until August 1945, in the process conducting 188 harrowing missions as part of the daylight campaign.

The 486th's initial mount was the redoubtable Liberator, decked out in the standard USAAF camouflage scheme of olive drab upper surfaces and neutral grey undersides. However, as we have seen, the Americans were more than adept at adding colour and individuality to their aircraft, and the 486th was no exception. The 834th squadron in particular was to achieve fame for the decoration of its bombers, thanks to the presence of Sgt Phil Brinkman, a former commercial artist who had worked in Chicago and St Louis. Even before the 834th had left the States, commanding officer Winfred D. Howell had noticed Brinkman's talent and officially attached him as a 'draftsman'. Howell also gave permission for his squadron's aircraft to be known as the 'Zodiacs', and once at Sudbury it became Brinkman's task to create twelve suitable nose art designs, in addition to other artistic activities around the base.

Unfortunately, the continual transfer of B24s between units, not to mention combat losses, meant that the 'Zodiac' project was never completed, being finally abandoned when the 486th transitioned to B17

Fortresses in August 1944. Nonetheless, Brinkman contributed some of most spectacular and original artwork to be seen anywhere in the Army Air Force.

Another notable personality attached to the 486th was Capt. Dick Grace, at age 46 the oldest operational pilot in the 8th AF. Surviving a full tour with the Group, he later transferred to the 448th BG at Seething before finally being ordered back to the USA.

The 486th suffered 33 combat losses and a further 24 to accidents – sadly, two of the latter came in May 1945 after hostilities had ceased, when two B17s collided on a training flight with the loss of both crews. After the Americans' departure Sudbury quickly fell out of use, and today the site is the usual mix of agriculture and light industry, though one of the former airfield buildings is now a café, offering a pleasant opportunity to contemplate the sacrifices of the past. Lingering affection for the young – and not so young – men who fought for a foreign land is evidenced by two memorials, one at the airfield site itself, the other within Sudbury church.

The view west across the airfield. The heavily modified T2 hangar, is just visible at centre. Part of the NW-SE runway is in the foreground.

Operational history

Mar 44 – Aug 45: 486th BG USAAF (B24H,J Liberator / B17G Flying Fortress – heavy bombing)

Location
S of Acton, W of Gt Waddingfield, N of B1115.   Grove Lane & Upthorpe
Road connect to Perimeter Track.

*The remarkably unassuming memorial to the 486th BG at Sudbury, located close
to the surviving hangar. It identifies the 486th as a USAF unit, even though the
United States Air Force did not come into existence until 1947 – the Air Force
was a division of the US Army throughout the Second World War.*

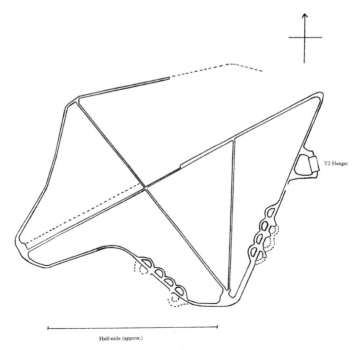

Half-mile (approx.)

TUDDENHAM

Physical fitness was an important factor in the airman's life. Seen here is the largely ruined gymnasium with its tell-tale chancel extension at left, while the taller building beyond was a Squash Court, to drawing 16589/40. These buildings are dispersed south of the main airfield site.

Tuddenham opened in October 1943, under the control of nearby Mildenhall, its first residents being 90 sqn who were to be the airfield's signature unit, remaining until late 1946. Prior to its arrival in Suffolk this outfit had occupied a wide variety of airfields and undertaken some unusual operations, including Bomber Command's disastrous flirtation with the American Flying Fortress. Now flying Stirling IIIs, they undertook a long campaign of mine-laying missions, interspersed with more high-profile raids such as attacks on V-weapon sites. 58 combat losses demonstrated how the Stirling remained very vulnerable as a heavy bomber.

In May 1944, 90 sqn – no doubt to their great relief – transitioned to the Lancaster. Attacks on rail centres and further V-weapon targets followed, before the squadron participated in daylight operations supporting the Normandy invasion. The squadron's 'C' flight was detached to form 186 sqn in October, and in March 1945, 138 sqn, a former Special Ops unit that had converted to the Lancaster, also arrived at Tuddenham.

In the immediate post-war years two more Lancaster squadrons took up residence, in anticipation of potential overseas service. However, the impression of a profusion of 'Lancs' would be misleading, given that by April 1946 all the squadrons were operating on barely half their previous strengths. In November heavy bombers left Tuddenham for good and the airfield closed to flying, although retained by the RAF.

In 1954 Tuddenham was passed to the USAF, but it was never again to see operational aircraft. Instead, in July 1959, 107sqn were installed with their flight of Thor nuclear missiles. These terrifying weapons remained until 1963 – the good news of their removal being tempered by the demise of Tuddenham as a military installation. Modern-day quarrying activity means that very little of the site survives, although 90 sqn are pleasingly commemorated by a sundial on the village green.

Part of the Perimeter Track, still just about discernible on the eastern side of the former airfield. The present-day quarry is just to the left of this view.

Operational history

Oct 43 – Nov 46: 90 sqn (Stirling III / Lancaster I,III – heavy bombing)
Oct 44 – Dec 44: 186 sqn (Lancaster I,III – heavy bombing)
Mar 45 – Nov 46: 138 sqn (Lancaster I,III – heavy bombing)
Apr 46 – Nov 46: 149 sqn (Lancaster I,III – heavy bombing)
Apr 46 – Nov 46: 207 sqn (Lancaster I,III – heavy bombing)
Jul 59 – Jul 63: 107 sqn (Thor IRBM – nuclear deterrent/strike)

Location

E of Tuddenham, N of Cavenham. Cavenham Road connects to fragment of Perimeter Track & remains of runway, which is now quarry access. Surviving buildings lie to the south of Cavenham Road.

Electrical Sub-station, one of the very few buildings still extant at Tuddenham – original RAF paintwork can be seen in the doorway. Note the intact blast walls.

WESTLEY

*Something of Westley's rustic nature is captured in this view, looking from the
south-west. The houses cover the former airfield site.*

Probably the least-known wartime airfield in Suffolk, Westley today eludes
the curious visitor, having disappeared decades ago beneath a housing
estate. Despite a brief operational life, the site has an intriguing history,
spotlighting the unsung activities of the little-regarded Army Co-Operation
Command.

The airfield opened in 1938 as a private strip belonging to the Suffolk
Aero Club. The club operated the Taylorcraft C, the military version of
which was known as the Auster and, in a neat twist, would play a
significant role in Westley's wartime career. As war loomed, the site was
deemed too small for either Civil Air Guard or Volunteer Reserve use, thus
at the outbreak of hostilities it was closed.

Army Co-Operation Command reactivated the field in 1940,
presumably because of its proximity to the large Bury barracks. The
quintessential Army Co-op aircraft was the Westland Lysander, before it
entered legend as the SOE's favoured 'taxi'. Later, the American-built

Curtiss Tomahawk – a fighter that had been quickly discarded by the RAF – took over the 'Lizzie's' role in patrolling the east coast for invading forces.

In August 1942 the first Air Observation Post squadron – no. 652 – arrived for training, initially with Tiger Moths but later transitioning to the Auster I. AOP squadrons would become greatly feared by German troops, as their function would be to spot ground forces and direct artillery fire to their location. Despite their lightness and slow speed, Austers were rugged birds and proved decidedly difficult to shoot down.

A second AOP squadron - no. 656 – was formed at Westley in December, eventually departing for India in the summer of 1943. Army Co-Operation Command officially disbanded in 1943, but Auster training continued at the site along with major exercises up until D-Day, at which point all flying abruptly ceased. Thus Westley, having played its small but vital part, was lost to history.

Operational history
Sep 40 – Apr 41: 268 sqn (Lysander II / Tomahawk – army co-operation)
Aug 42 – Jan 43: 652 sqn (Taylorcraft Plus C.2 / Tiger Moth / Auster I – Air
Observation Post)
Dec 42 – Mar 43: 656 sqn (Tiger Moth / Auster I,III – Air Observation Post)
May 43 – Jun 43: 657 sqn (Auster III – Air Observation Post)
Feb 44 – Jun 44: 662 sqn (Auster III,IV – Air Observation Post

Location
W of Bury town centre, off A1302 Newmarket road.

WOODBRIDGE

Denuded of aerials and external fittings, Woodbridge's Control Tower overlooks a field increasingly colonised by wild flowers.

As has been noted throughout this volume, bomber units of both the RAF and USAAF suffered heavy losses to causes other than direct enemy action. On any flight, landing is the most dangerous phase, and on day and night missions this danger was heightened by factors such as combat damage, crew fatigue, fuel shortage and poor weather. By 1942, with the bombing campaign entering its most intensive phase, a clear need was identified for dedicated Emergency Landing Grounds for heavy bombers, and three sites were earmarked – Carnaby, Manston and Woodbridge.

When construction began in July 1942 it was obvious that Woodbridge was not going to be a conventional airfield. It was carved out of forestry land, and an estimated one million trees were sacrificed in the process: the appeal of the site was its coastal proximity and a relatively fog-free climate. One massive runway was laid, 3,000yds long and 250yds wide, with 500yd overshoots at each end. The runway was sub-divided into three lanes, one of which was reserved for the direst emergencies – no permission was required to make a landing on this section. If and when fog did appear, the airfield was equipped with the scary but effective FIDO fog dispersal system, and a complex array of runway lighting was installed and refined throughout Woodbridge's wartime career.

Cold War structures upon WW2 foundations at Woodbridge: at left a partially sunken Sentry Post with a Weapons Discharge Area visible beyond, and three Hardened Aircraft Shelters at centre. The heavily overgrown area in between is the eastern overshoot from the huge single runway.

Woodbridge became operational in November 1943 and hosted 36 landings in its first month: 60 aircraft arrived in January 1944, and 72 in February, of which 48 were USAAF. During May the tally rose to 150 landings, and in October there were an astounding 360. The harrowing nature of operations at Woodbridge is illustrated by the events of June 22nd: three Lancasters, one of them still carrying 11,000 lbs of bombs, and a B17 all crash-landed within a thirteen-minute span. One particularly welcome, but most unexpected landing occurred on 13th July, when a Junkers Ju88G night-fighter, lost and low on fuel, inadvertently touched down at Woodbridge. Its capture provided vital information on German air-interception radar.

A brief hiatus in Woodbridge's grim but vital operations came in March 1945, when Halifax glider tugs, with Hamilcar and Horsa assault gliders, were deployed to the field for participation in Operation Varsity, the Rhine crossing. Then it was back to business as usual, and by the close of hostilities Woodbridge had accommodated a phenomenal 4,120 landings, making it by far the busiest of the dedicated emergency airfields.

This Watch Tower overlooked the Weapons Storage Area at Woodbridge, manned by armed Guards around the clock, and generally operated on a 'shoot first, ask questions later' basis.

However, this was not to be the end for such a magnificent aviation venue. In 1952 the USAF took over the site, developing it into a Cold War nexus, eventually 'twinned' with nearby Bentwaters. The 81st Tactical Fighter Wing arrived in June 1958 and remained until the base closed in 1993. In 1969 the 67th ARRS brought its formidable rescue assets, comprising HC130 Hercules transports and HH53E 'Jolly Green Giant' helicopters. Today the site clings on to military aviation, being used occasionally by the Army Air Corps for exercises and training deployments from Wattisham. Establishment of an army barracks has, sadly, led to a number of buildings being demolished. However, the huge runway survives, although only the central strip is now maintained, and it is intriguing to consider how this vast swathe of battered concrete would have been such a welcome sight to the brave fliers of WW2.

Operational history

Aug 44:   149 sqn★ (Lancaster I,III – heavy bombing)

Oct 52 – Jan 70: 20th FBW USAF (F84G Thunderstreak / F100 Super Sabre – strike)

Jun 58 – Aug 93: 81st TFW USAF (F84F Thunderstreak / F101 Voodoo / F4D Phantom II / A10A Thunderbolt II – tactical fighter ops)

Dec 69 – Apr 92: 67th ARRS USAF (HC130 Hercules / HH53E – air-sea rescue)

★detachment only

Location

SE of Bromeswell, S of B1084. Minor road to Tangham & Capel St Andrew passes eastern end of site.

Specially marked Hardened Aircraft Shelter commemorates its final resident, the A-10 Thunderbolt II

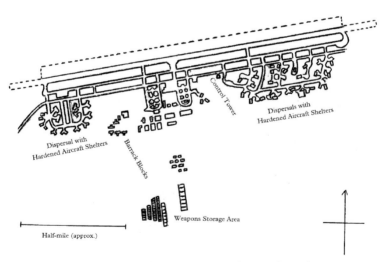

Note: This plan is greatly simplified in order to show only major structures and general layout. Comparison with the 'twin' base at Bentwaters is instructive; there, the original WW2 three-runway layout was progressively overlain with a Jet Age single-runway installation; at Woodbridge, no such alterations were necessary, giving the impression that the site was purpose-built for Cold War operations.

123

These sinister-looking buildings were fortified shelters for fuel trucks, aka 'bowsers'.

A long view of Woodbridge's colossal runway, taken from among the approach lights at the eastern end. The vast sea of concrete was the last hope for many a weary, wounded crew.

Memorial arch once in place at Woodbridge's sports stadium, now in the care of Bentwaters Cold War Museum. Col. Dorman was a former commander of the 81st TFW, who was shot down and killed during the Vietnam War. The stadium no longer exists, but the author has fond recollections of the venue, having watched the Bentwaters Phantoms football team host the Alconbury Spartans in the late 1980s. The teams, like their respective bases, are consigned to memory.

A formidable pillbox installation guarding the southern approaches to Woodbridge airfield. It now overlooks a major road junction.